Interviewing Vulnerable Suspects

This book is an in-depth, evidence-based guide to interviewing suspects with specific vulnerabilities. It provides an overview of current research, practices, and legal considerations for interviewing vulnerable suspects, incorporating guidelines regarding the identification of vulnerabilities, engaging with third parties in the interview, and training and supervision. It then goes on to cover specific vulnerabilities typically encountered in suspect populations, providing clear summaries of current research, case studies, and practical guidance for conducting interviews with these populations to facilitate best practice in interviewing. Expertise is drawn from both law enforcement practice and academic research to ensure an evidence-based approach that is relevant for contemporary practice.

Interviewing Vulnerable Suspects offers the international policing audience a practical guide to interviewing vulnerable suspects for both uniform police and detectives. It is relevant for statutory bodies involved in investigations of misconduct; legal practitioners and forensic psychologists; practitioners in counselling, social work, and psychology; and students in policing, criminology, and forensic psychology programs.

Jane Tudor-Owen is an Honorary Lecturer in the Discipline of Psychology and Criminology at Edith Cowan University in Perth, Western Australia, and a practising lawyer. As an academic, her primary area of research is investigative interviewing.

Celine van Golde is a Senior Lecturer at the University of Sydney in New South Wales, Australia. Her primary research focus is on the reliability of memory in children and adults, specifically how interviewing techniques, such as those used by police, lawyers, and judges, can affect memory accuracy.

Ray Bull is (part time) Professor of Criminal Investigation at Derby University, UK. His main topic of expertise is investigative interviewing and he has been invited to give presentations on this in dozens of countries. He has written expert reports in around 200 cases and testified in over 20.

David Gee (MBE) is a former Head of CID in the Derbyshire Police and has held numerous national lead roles, most notably on the investigation and prosecution of sex offences, homicide review, and as advisor to the Home Office and ACPO (now NPCC) on the investigation of rape.

Contributor **Becky Milne** is Professor of Forensic Psychology at the University of Portsmouth, UK, is a chartered forensic psychologist and scientist, and Associate Fellow of the British Psychological Society. The main focus of her work over the past 25 years concerns the examination of police interviewing and investigation. Jointly with practitioners, she has helped to develop procedures to improve the quality of interviews of witnesses, victims, intelligence sources, and suspects of crime internationally.

Routledge Series on Practical and Evidence-Based Policing

Books in the Routledge Series on Practical and Evidence-Based Policing disseminate knowledge and provide practical tools for law enforcement leaders and personnel to protect and serve the public and reduce crime. With an aim to bridge the "translation gap" between frontline policing and academic research, books in this series apply sound scientific methods as well as practical experience to make everyday police work safer and smarter. These books are an invaluable resource for police practitioners, academic researchers, public policymakers, and students in law enforcement and criminology programs to guide best practices in all aspects of policing.

Police Misconduct Complaint Investigations Manual, 2nd Edition
Barbara Attard & Kathryn Olson

Police and YOUth
Everette B. Penn & Shannon A. Davenport

Twenty-One Mental Models for Policing
A Framework for Using Data and Research for Overcoming Cognitive Bias
Renée J. Mitchell

Public Corruption in the United States
Analysis of a Destructive Phenomenon
Jeff Cortese

The Wicked Problems of Police Reform in Canada
Laura Huey, Lorna Ferguson & Jennifer L. Schulenberg

Human Rights Policing
Reimagining Law Enforcement in the 21st Century
Peter Marina & Pedro Marina

Interviewing Vulnerable Suspects
Safeguarding the Process
Edited by Jane Tudor-Owen, Celine van Golde, Ray Bull, & David Gee

Interviewing Vulnerable Suspects

Safeguarding the Process

Edited by Jane Tudor-Owen, Celine van Golde, Ray Bull, and David Gee

NEW YORK AND LONDON

Designed cover image: © Mart van Golde

First published 2023
by Routledge
605 Third Avenue, New York, NY 10158

and by Routledge
4 Park Square, Milton Park, Abingdon, Oxon, OX14 4RN

Routledge is an imprint of the Taylor & Francis Group, an informa business

© 2023 selection and editorial matter, Jane Tudor-Owen, Celine van Golde, Ray Bull, and David Gee; individual chapters, the contributors

The right of Jane Tudor-Owen, Celine van Golde, Ray Bull, and David Gee to be identified as the authors of the editorial material, and of the authors for their individual chapters, has been asserted in accordance with sections 77 and 78 of the Copyright, Designs and Patents Act 1988.

All rights reserved. No part of this book may be reprinted or reproduced or utilised in any form or by any electronic, mechanical, or other means, now known or hereafter invented, including photocopying and recording, or in any information storage or retrieval system, without permission in writing from the publishers.

Trademark notice: Product or corporate names may be trademarks or registered trademarks, and are used only for identification and explanation without intent to infringe.

ISBN: 978-0-367-70379-0 (hbk)
ISBN: 978-0-367-70168-0 (pbk)
ISBN: 978-1-003-14599-8 (ebk)

DOI: 10.4324/9781003145998

Typeset in Bembo
by Deanta Global Publishing Services, Chennai, India

Contents

Acknowledgements — vii

Introduction — 1

PART I

1 Vulnerability: The bigger picture — 7
JANE TUDOR-OWEN AND CELINE VAN GOLDE

2 Identifying vulnerability: The importance of planning and rapport — 12
JANE TUDOR-OWEN AND CELINE VAN GOLDE

3 Interviewing with a third party — 19
JANE TUDOR-OWEN AND CELINE VAN GOLDE

4 Training interviewers — 24
RAY BULL AND BECKY MILNE

5 Interview supervision and management — 34
RAY BULL AND BECKY MILNE

PART II

6 Interviewing intoxicated suspects — 45
CELINE VAN GOLDE, JANE TUDOR-OWEN, AND DAVID GEE

7 Interviewing older adult suspects — 52
CELINE VAN GOLDE, JANE TUDOR-OWEN, AND DAVID GEE

8 Children as suspects — 58
CELINE VAN GOLDE, JANE TUDOR-OWEN, AND DAVID GEE

9 Interviewing suspects with mental illness — 65
JANE TUDOR-OWEN, CELINE VAN GOLDE, AND DAVID GEE

10	Interviewing suspects with intellectual and learning impairments CELINE VAN GOLDE, JANE TUDOR-OWEN, AND DAVID GEE	72
11	Culturally and Linguistically Diverse (CaLD) and First Nations suspects CELINE VAN GOLDE, JANE TUDOR-OWEN, AND DAVID GEE	80
12	Interviewing in the context of gender and sexual diversity JANE TUDOR-OWEN, CELINE VAN GOLDE, AND DAVID GEE	89
13	Interviewing suspects with a hearing impairment CELINE VAN GOLDE, JANE TUDOR-OWEN, AND DAVID GEE	95

Conclusion 103
Index 106

Acknowledgements

This book would not have been completed without the support and assistance of many individuals around the world. The editors gratefully acknowledge the following individuals for their contribution (in alphabetical order): Peter Addison (Cleveland Police), Jamal Barnes, Adam Ebell, James McCue, Becky Milne, Mart van Golde, David Waters, Craig Williamson, and Andrew Wilson.

Introduction

The aim of an investigative interview is to ascertain the truth. To avoid miscarriages of justice, investigators must ensure fairness and voluntariness in interviews. This is made more challenging with regard to some suspects by the impact of vulnerabilities. As these vulnerabilities are often not visible, they can be difficult to identify, particularly without specialised training. The vulnerabilities that may impact a suspect's ability to engage in an interview may be on the basis of physical, psychological, and cultural differences, each bringing specific considerations in terms of identification, as well as requirements to modify the interview itself.

The concept of admissibility is at the core of considering vulnerability in the context of a police interview. However, vulnerability will not be examined from a strictly legal perspective in this book. The law, in many jurisdictions around the world, is clear on this: fairness to the accused is paramount. The argument, therefore, will be whether, in regard to all the circumstances, the accused has been treated fairly. Rather than examining the legalities concerning the point at which an interview will be considered inadmissible on a fairness basis, the focus of this book is ensuring police are equipped to make interviews as fair as possible, leaving the courts to determine issues of admissibility.

The starting point for this handbook is an acknowledgement of the difficult work undertaken by police and other professionals in the criminal justice system. The motivation for this book came from an awareness that police (and others) are mindful of the importance of safeguarding interviews with vulnerable suspects, but do not necessarily have the knowledge or skills to do so. Training is only now catching up with advances in understanding the particular ways vulnerability can impact interviewing, and the vast majority of police officers are not formally trained in diagnosing vulnerability of any kind.

Of course it would be easier if vulnerabilities were discrete; however, there is much overlap. That is, one suspect may have multiple vulnerabilities that impact each other. A good example is considering a 15-year-old First Nations suspect diagnosed with Foetal Alcohol Spectrum Disorder (FASD). A police officer would need to consider the age, culture, and FASD diagnosis in preparing for that interview. To that end, while this book treats the vulnerabilities covered in Part II discretely, there is benefit in reading across the text to have an overview of the various ways in which vulnerability can impact interviewing and how specific vulnerabilities may co-exist or be interrelated. The investigative interviewing model, PEACE (examined in detail in Chapter 4), has been found to be suitable for use with vulnerable populations. However, throughout this text, we provide guidelines for modifying standard interview procedures to promote fairness for people with specific vulnerabilities. Many of the suggestions are applicable across specific vulnerabilities, and we would say they are good practice generally to ensure fairness, particularly given that many vulnerabilities are invisible.

DOI: 10.4324/9781003145998-1

In Australia, the case of *Anunga v R* (1976) 11 ALR 412, establishes the importance of considering vulnerability in police interviewing (in that case specific reference is made to interviewing Aboriginal and Torres Strait Islander peoples):

> It may be thought by some that these guidelines are unduly paternal and therefore offensive to Aboriginal people. It may be thought by others that they are unduly favourable to Aboriginal people. The truth of the matter is they are designed simply to remove or obviate some of the disadvantages from which Aboriginal people suffer in dealings with police. These guidelines are not absolute rules, departure from which will necessarily lead to statements being excluded, but police officers who depart from them without reason may find statements excluded.
>
> (*Anunga v R* (1976) 11 ALR 412, per Forster J at 415)

It is in this spirit that this book is presented: as an avenue through which to understand more about the ways in which vulnerability generally, and particular vulnerabilities specifically, can impact on the fairness of a police interview. By understanding more, appropriate adjustments can be made to ensure the most just outcome for all involved.

Structure of the book

This book is separated into two parts. The first part provides an overview of current research, practices, and legal considerations for interviewing vulnerable suspects, incorporating guidelines regarding the identification of vulnerabilities, engaging with third parties in the interview, and training and supervision. The second part of this book examines specific vulnerabilities individually, providing clear summaries of current research and practical guidance for conducting interviews with these populations to facilitate best practice in interviewing. In some chapters, case studies are included to provide examples of the way in which particular vulnerabilities, or vulnerability more generally, is being addressed in jurisdictions around the world.

Part I

Part I of this book addresses the general considerations with respect to vulnerability and provides a foundation from which to consider the impact of specific vulnerabilities addressed in Part II. Chapter 1 discusses the concept of vulnerability, and highlights the need to consider the extent to which a person is vulnerable by virtue of their contact with the criminal justice system, in addition to any specific vulnerabilities that may be relevant to them. Chapter 2 discusses the important role of rapport and planning in identifying and accommodating vulnerability in interviews. Having considered the way vulnerability might be identified, Chapter 3 examines the use of third parties (intermediaries, lawyers, and interpreters) in interviews to promote fairness. Chapter 4 provides an overview of investigative interviewing and its applicability and adaptability for interviewing vulnerable suspects, and Chapter 5 establishes the importance of supervision in introducing, developing, and maintaining skills in interviewing.

Part II

Part II of this book provides an overview of specific vulnerabilities and the way in which they may impact a police interview when present. Chapter 6 discusses interviewing intoxicated suspects, including alcohol and other drugs, recognising the impact of prescription drug use on interviews. Chapter 7 considers the impact of older age on interviews, including reference to Alzheimer's Disease and Dementia, and Chapter 8 considers the impact of age at the other end of the spectrum—interviewing children as suspects. Recognising the increasing exposure of police to people experiencing mental illness, in Chapter 9 we explore the ways in which a suspect's mental illness can impact the fairness of a police interview. Similarly, Chapter 10 discusses the impact of intellectual and learning impairments and those that are related, such as FASD and Autism Spectrum Disorder (ASD). Acknowledging the breadth of this area, in Chapter 11 we attempt to consider the ways that being Culturally and Linguistically Diverse or a member of a First Nations people group can be a vulnerability in the context of police interviews. Chapter 12 discusses the historical relationship between police and gender- and/or sexually-diverse suspects and the implications of this for interviewing, along with strategies to promote inclusion. Finally, Chapter 13 provides guidelines for interviewing suspects with hearing impairments, recognising this is not confined to older adult suspects and is further complicated by the use of interpreters.

We trust the information covered in this book will be a useful guide when you are working with vulnerable suspects. We are aware that there are other vulnerabilities that you might encounter, but believe that the guidelines provided are good practice generally to ensure fairness of the interview for all those involved.

IV

Part I

Chapter 1

Vulnerability
The bigger picture

Jane Tudor-Owen and Celine van Golde

Executive summary

In this chapter, the concept of vulnerability is explored in detail, providing a starting point from which to examine specific aspects of interviewing relevant to interviewing vulnerable suspects. The chapter then goes on to examine the impact of specific vulnerabilities on the interviewing process. After which the impact of specific vulnerabilities on the interviewing process will be examined.

Introduction

The uncomfortable truth is that vulnerability can serve a purpose for those in power within the criminal justice system. If suspects are feeling vulnerable, they may be more likely to acquiesce and be compliant. On the face of it, this is not a bad thing. However, if that compliance results in a person not exercising their rights, or them agreeing to things that are not true (e.g., a false confession), then there is a problem. Increasing attention is being paid to vulnerability by some criminal justice systems, from both practical and conceptual perspectives (Bartkowiak-Théron et al., 2017) and, perhaps unsurprisingly, the consensus is that vulnerability is a complicated concept (e.g., Bartkowiak-Théron et al., 2017; Cummins, 2014).

A popular principle within most criminal justice systems around the world is that all people are considered equal before the law. Unfortunately, this can lead to the mistaken belief that everyone must be treated the same (Fineman, 2010). However, at this point, it is important to acknowledge that vulnerability is often defined by people who are not (perceived as) vulnerable themselves, and the very people who may be characterised as vulnerable may not identify with the label assigned to them (Bartkowiak-Théron et al., 2017). The extent to which an individual identifies as someone who might be categorised as vulnerable for the purposes of specific policies and procedures is relevant in understanding individual autonomy. In the context of policing, it also raises important questions about admissibility if an individual who would typically be categorised as vulnerable does not self-identify as such, and does not wish to be treated differently to the general population. The balance between respecting autonomy and adherence to policy is a prominent concern.

Even when adopting a narrow definition of vulnerability, based purely on innate characteristics and features of the individual (e.g., diagnosed mental illness), social structure plays a significant role in determining vulnerability. It is widely acknowledged that the disproportionate interaction between vulnerable people and the criminal justice system is, at least in part, caused by the deinstitutionalisation of mental health services (keeping mentally ill people in the communities rather than in hospitals), and punitive responses to manifestations of mental illness (Cummins, 2014). Certainly, deinstitutionalisation has resulted in increasing contact

DOI: 10.4324/9781003145998-3

between police and people with mental health concerns. Therefore, regardless of whether vulnerability is conceptualised narrowly or broadly, institutions, and the actors within them, have a role to play in reducing the risk of harm to people who are vulnerable.

This chapter will firstly explore different understandings of vulnerability, then examine how vulnerability is defined and operationalised in legislation, policy, and procedure governing police interactions. The importance of recognising vulnerability more broadly in the context of the criminal justice system will then be discussed, including some practical considerations for the policing context.

Conceptualising vulnerability

Vulnerability has been explored across disciplines, providing a rich understanding when discussing vulnerability in the context of the criminal justice system. In the literature, it is conceptualised variously as innate characteristics at the individual level and/or as being universal, resulting in the need for some sort of assistance. Asquith and Bartkowiak-Théron (2021) note four types of vulnerability relevant to police work: ontological (fragility by virtue of being human); individual (vulnerability due to individual characteristics); situational (due to the circumstances in which one finds themselves); and iatrogenic (vulnerability further exacerbated through contact with police). The current approach to recognising and accounting for vulnerability in the policing context will be examined first, before then turning attention to the way in which the universal approach might be used to complement existing frameworks.

Vulnerability in the criminal justice system

Internationally, special classes of vulnerability are recognised in legislation, policy, and procedure used throughout criminal justice systems. Although the focus of this book is police interviewing, there can be no argument against the notion that the interview itself is impacted by what precedes it, regardless of where the interaction might lie on the spectrum, from an invitation to attend a police station through to a high profile and public arrest.

The way vulnerability is defined across the various points at which a person might encounter the criminal justice system provides insight into the approach more generally of that jurisdiction. Further, it is helpful to see the extent to which definitions are consistent both across and within jurisdictions. In their examination of how vulnerability is considered in the legislation in England and Wales, Dehaghani (2020) notes the difference in the scope of vulnerability recognised in the *Police and Criminal Evidence Act 1984* Code C pre- and post-2018. Rather than limiting the definition of vulnerability to defined classes of people (under 18, and issues with understanding due to mental capacity), the criteria introduced in the 2018 amendment instead refers to "understanding and communication in relation to rights, entitlements, procedures and processes, clarity of thought, and suggestibility and acquiescence" (Dehaghani, 2020, p. 2).

Scholars in the psycho-legal context have typically defined vulnerability in terms of characteristics that may render a person more likely to have difficulty understanding their interactions with police, their rights, and/or the implications of what they say, than someone not experiencing those same stressors (Dehaghani, 2020). Someone deemed "vulnerable" is generally categorised as such "because they possess an individual or social characteristic that is known to bring about disadvantage, such as age, indigeneity, mental illness, race/ethnicity, cognitive impairment, disability, homelessness, sexuality and/or gender identity, or addiction" (Bartkowiak-Théron et al., 2017, p. 2; Bartkowiak-Théron & Asquith, 2012). Police are generally known to have focused primarily on the first four, with special dispensation built into policy and procedure noting that individuals with these characteristics should be treated differently from the general population (Bartkowiak-Théron et al., 2017).

This approach to vulnerability that requires membership of discrete groups is referred to as "siloed" and is criticised due to the risk that an individual's experience is misrecognised (Bartkowiak-Théron et al., 2017). Additionally, it leaves police with increasing numbers of operating procedures to consider in isolation (Bartkowiak-Théron & Asquith, 2012). It is also important to recognise that although police are coming into contact with greater numbers of people who are vulnerable by virtue of innate characteristics (as mentioned above), training in this area for police is still lacking (Cummins, 2014). As Bartkowiak-Théron and colleagues (2017) suggest, "with each new vulnerability attribute added to the normative list of recognisable vulnerabilities, policies and practices become increasingly maladapted to the task of remedying those vulnerabilities" (p. 5).

Thinking about vulnerability more broadly

There is an emerging school of thought that considers vulnerability as universal, in that it affects us all (Bartkowiak-Théron et al., 2017; Fineman, 2010) and recognises that there are unequal power dynamics between police (the State) and suspects (Dehaghani, 2019). This conceptualisation does not mean there cannot be specific vulnerabilities; vulnerability can be a result of innate or situational characteristics or a combination of both (Dehaghani, 2020). An analysis of vulnerability must therefore consider the individual and societal relationships (Fineman, 2010). Innate characteristics include those things that are specific to the person; for example, personality characteristics and mental disorders (encompassing mental illness, learning, and intellectual disabilities). In contrast, situational characteristics include life experience, recent events, the features of the crime itself (if the suspect was involved), and the experience of being in contact with the criminal justice system. At present, the majority of agency guidance regarding vulnerability focuses on the innate characteristics and tends to ignore situational characteristics (Dehaghani, 2020). In the worst cases, the context of interviewing actually exacerbates the vulnerability caused by situational factors. A universal understanding of vulnerability places responsibility on institutions and structures to be responsive to individuals' collective vulnerability (Bartkowiak-Théron et al., 2017), as well as particular vulnerabilities.

Inadequate responses to universal vulnerability can further serve to compound the harm experienced by those labelled as vulnerable (Bartkowiak-Théron et al., 2017). Focusing exclusively on individual characteristics as the diagnostic tool for identifying someone as vulnerable is also problematic as it diverts attention away from the ways in which the environment and, more broadly, social structures can be modified to improve the experience of vulnerable people. It also assumes that vulnerability is visible, when in reality it can be either intentionally, or unintentionally, concealed (Coliandris, 2015). The only factors impacting the vulnerability of suspects that police have control over are situational. That is, from the time the suspect first has contact with the police until they are released or remanded in custody. The processes by which a suspect is initially identified, detained, and questioned each provide opportunities to either increase or decrease the vulnerability of this suspect. Importantly, it is not only the interactions with people, but also the impact of the environment in which the suspect finds themselves.

Being in police custody can promote vulnerability through isolation, lack of control, and uncertainty, which can be further exacerbated by ignorance of the law (Dehaghani, 2020). These factors can also be relevant for individuals attending voluntarily to assist police with their enquiries. In applying Fineman's vulnerability theory, Dehaghani (2020) suggests it is not one group or specific groups of individuals who are vulnerable but rather that all suspects are vulnerable and that it is the circumstances of the police custodial process, investigative process and wider criminal process that deplete or decrease resilience.

(p. 13)

This approach removes the focus from individual characteristics and instead considers environmental and structural opportunities for change.

Addressing contextual vulnerability in a policing context

Addressing contextual vulnerability requires that attention be paid to those factors impacting the resilience of individuals: isolation, lack of control, uncertainty, and ignorance of the law (Dehaghani, 2020). Some degree of isolation is unavoidable; however, by minimising the use of custody to situations of last resort and ensuring the availability of access to a support person the extent of isolation could be reduced. This access may be provided via phone or in cases where there are personal vulnerabilities that need to be considered, this might be in person, particularly in an interview, for example, an interview friend or an appropriate adult. Certainly, for suspects who speak a language other than English, the provision of an interpreter is also likely to reduce the feeling of isolation both prior to and during an interview (discussed further in Chapter 3—Interviewing with a Third Party, Chapter 11—Culturally and Linguistically Diverse (CaLD) and First Nations Suspects, and Chapter 13—Interviewing Suspects with a Hearing Impairment).

In their article examining ways in which to reframe vulnerability in a policing context, Dehaghani (2020) provides the following suggestions:

- Clear and frequent communication from police to assist suspects to feel they have more control and minimise their uncertainty. The lack of control experienced by most suspects (also victims and witnesses, to a lesser extent) may serve a purpose if it disorients the individual and encourages compliance. The reality remains: the suspect is not in control. However, making the suspect aware of their rights regularly (recognising that cognitive load may mean they need to be reminded) can provide some sense of control.
- Providing a road map to suspects at each stage of the process will also decrease feelings of uncertainty. While it is impossible to say with any certainty what will happen, giving as much detail as possible about what to expect, and possible outcomes, will allay some level of anxiety caused by uncertainty.
- Public education about police policy and procedure, demystifying the process, may also assist in building suspects' resilience when they do come into contact with the criminal justice system. This would seem to be particularly important for younger suspects who may not have critically analysed media representations of policing and may subsequently be unnecessarily concerned; for example, about possible police brutality.

Conclusion

Although there is an argument for replacing the narrow definition of vulnerability that seems to plague legislation, policy, and procedure within the criminal justice system, and policing more specifically, doing so would be problematic from a practical perspective. An alternative, allowing for policy addressing specific characteristics that may afford safeguards to accommodate particular vulnerabilities, would be to expand the current, narrow definition and adopt the position that all people encountering the criminal justice system should be considered vulnerable as a starting point. In this way, the state must take responsibility for responding to the vulnerability of its members (Fineman, 2017).

Awareness of the special vulnerability of some classes of suspect has led to safeguards being adopted throughout some criminal justice systems. The purpose of this chapter is to examine vulnerability more generally; however, later chapters will explore the use of appropriate adults, interview friends, interpreters, and lawyers as further safeguards within the interview (Chapter 3) and the way in which the "PEACE" model of interviewing has safeguards inbuilt to reduce the influences of unskilled interviewing such as suggestive questioning (Chapter 4).

Whether vulnerability is pre-existing, a result of the event, and/or exacerbated by criminal justice institutions or the actors within, the costs of ignorance in terms of both monetary and social value should ensure greater attention is paid to ways in which it can be mitigated. Active work to increase the resilience of suspects through attention to both innate characteristics and situational characteristics will in turn reduce the likelihood of miscarriages of justice (Bartkowiak-Théron et al., 2017) as well as increase appropriate convictions.

References

Asquith, N.L., & Bartkowiak-Théron, I. (2021). *Policing practices and vulnerable people*. Springer. eBook.

Bartkowiak-Théron, I. & Asquith, N.L. (2012). The extraordinary intricacies of policing vulnerability. *Australasian Policing, 4*, 43–49.

Bartkowiak-Théron, I., Asquith, N.L., & Roberts, K.A. (2017). *Policing encounters with vulnerability*. Palgrave Macmillan, eBook.

Coliandris, G. (2015). County lines and wicked problems: Exploring the need for improved policing approaches to vulnerability and early intervention. *Australasian Policing, 7*, 25–35.

Cummins, I. (2014). Policing, custody and mental illness. In Sheehan, R., & Ogloff, J. (Eds.), *Working within the forensic paradigm: Cross-discipline approaches for policy and practice* (pp. 167–182).

Dehaghani, R. (2019). The (vulnerable) suspect in the criminal process. In Dehaghani, R. (Ed.), *Vulnerability in police custody: Police decision-making and the appropriate adult safeguard*. Routledge, eBook.

Dehaghani, R. (2021). Interrogating vulnerability: Reframing the vulnerable suspect in police custody. *Social and Legal Studies, 30*(2), 251–271. doi: 10.1177/0964663920921921

Fineman, M.A. (2010). The vulnerable subject and the responsive state. *Emory Law Journal, 60*, 251–276.

Fineman, M.A. (2017). Vulnerability and inevitable inequality. *Oslo Law Review, 4*, 133–149.

Chapter 2

Identifying vulnerability
The importance of planning and rapport

Jane Tudor-Owen and Celine van Golde

Executive summary

In this chapter, planning and rapport building are introduced as key to identifying vulnerability. Research has established that planning, as well as rapport building and maintenance, is important in ensuring positive outcomes in investigative interviews. It is also an avenue through which vulnerability can be identified. This chapter will canvass practical skills to facilitate planning and building rapport for the purpose of identifying vulnerability.

Introduction

The focus of Chapter 1 was exploring the idea that all suspects are vulnerable, to an extent, by virtue of their contact with the criminal justice system. In Part II of this book, there is an examination of the way in which particular characteristics of an individual further exacerbate that vulnerability. Previous literature has generally focused on psychological vulnerability; for example, mental illness and intellectual impairment, as these can certainly render a suspect at risk in the interview process. These characteristics are also addressed in this book (Chapters 9 and 10, respectively), in recognition of their importance. However, these are not the only characteristics that can impact the likelihood of a person requiring safeguarding in the interview and, in addition to those, this book examines suspects' intoxication, age (older adults and children), cultural and linguistic diversity, gender and sexual diversity, and physical disability (hearing impairment).

Central to the ability to adapt the interview process for the purposes of safeguarding is to be able to identify when a suspect is vulnerable as a result of a particular characteristic (or characteristics, as the case may be). Sometimes, this might be obvious. For example, a person of advanced age is likely to appear so. However, this example also highlights the take-home message which is that vulnerability is often invisible. While some persons of advanced age may have retained their cognitive capacity and would likely require less consideration on that basis, others may have experienced significant cognitive decline. The presence of "invisible" vulnerability requires police and other practitioners to engage in a process by which any relevant characteristics impacting the interview process are identified both before and during interviews.

There are a number of strategies that can be adopted, requiring varying levels of expertise. With regard to psychological vulnerability, some policing jurisdictions have adopted a universal screening approach (discussed in more detail in Chapters 9 and 10). Screening of that type is limited in its use with regard to other characteristics that are relevant in determining a suspect's potential vulnerabilities. When these are not apparent or unclear, it can be argued

DOI: 10.4324/9781003145998-4

that rapport building is the most useful tool in identifying whether a suspect may have a particular vulnerability.

On the face of it, rapport building may seem too simple to be of much use in identifying vulnerability. However, rapport building can be challenging in contexts where the parties are not in agreement (e.g., interviews with suspects) and it takes time. In the health domain, students and clinicians interviewed about patient communication cited limited time and chaotic settings as influencing their interactions, and noted the difficulty building rapport while trying to stay focused (Gilligan et al., 2021). When patient characteristics differed from their own and/or patients were reluctant to engage, this further impacted on the clinician's ability to build rapport (Gilligan et al., 2021). However, investigative interviewing research has found that rapport-based interviewing can be trained, resulting in increased perceptions of rapport by interviewees (Brimbal et al., 2021), and that adopting a rapport-based approach is associated with a larger amount of reported information (Holmberg & Madsen, 2014; Walsh & Bull, 2012). It will be further suggested that rapport building provides the opportunity to identify vulnerability.

The reason we have incorporated a discussion of the importance of interview planning into this chapter specifically is because it is inextricably intertwined with identifying vulnerability and with rapport building. Careful planning can inform strategies for building rapport, and rapport building can, in turn, inform planning.

In this chapter, the relevance of planning will be discussed before attention turns to rapport building. Components of rapport building will be discussed in a generic sense, followed by the findings of research examining rapport building in investigative interviews. The chapter will conclude by exploring strategies to build rapport in investigative interviews.

Relevance of planning

No interview is the same as another. Some suspects have a long history with police, while others have none. Where there is a file of information relating to a suspect, familiarity with the contents of the file may provide material to use in building rapport, and it may further identify vulnerabilities that will need to be taken into account in planning the interview. However, if there is no such file, or the contents of the file is limited, the time spent with the suspect prior to the interview (e.g., the arrest and processing) may afford an opportunity to learn more about them which can then be used to facilitate rapport building.

Clarke et al. (2011) suggested that a number of poor interviewing practices which were present prior to the implementation of the PEACE model can be attributed to insufficient planning. These practices included an inability to establish relevant facts, poor questioning technique, and inappropriate repetitive questioning. In their assessment of the PEACE model, Gudjonsson states, "there is clearly a strong emphasis on proper preparation prior to interviews, and on fairness and integrity during interviewing" (1994, p. 239). Within the "Preparation and planning" phase, Gudjonsson (1994) suggests there are seven principles for interviewers to consider: understanding why the interview is being conducted; identifying objectives; articulating the relevant elements of the offence(s); reviewing evidence already gathered; determining what evidence may still be available that has not been obtained; understanding the legislative and procedural requirements governing the interview; and ensuring the interview is designed with flexibility in mind. With respect to these principles, it may further be added that interviewers also need to turn their mind to any possible vulnerabilities and how they might be dealt with in an interview.

It may also be the case that during the "Engage and explain" phase of the interview, through rapport building, the interviewers become aware of vulnerabilities that need to be considered further. In those circumstances, it would be appropriate to pause the interview and take a break to discuss a plan for how to proceed with the other interviewer.

Components of rapport building

Rapport in its most basic form refers to a relationship between two people for the purpose of reporting information (Driskell et al., 2013). Rapport building is used across professions to build working relationships (Abbe & Brandon, 2013). A popular conceptualisation of rapport building identifies three components: mutual attentiveness; positivity; and coordination (Tickle-Degnen & Rosenthal, 1990). Mutual attentiveness is the focus of attention being on the other person in the interaction; positivity can include friendliness or caring; and coordination refers to the extent to which the parties are "in sync" with each other (Tickle-Degnen & Rosenthal, 1990). These components, together, contribute to building rapport. They will not necessarily be present in equal measure and, depending on the context, this is to be expected. These are also not static components and will change over time, or across interactions. For example, in an interview with a suspect you are unlikely to be in sync initially, although this may change as the interview progresses.

In recent research utilising Tickle-Degnan and Rosenthal's (1990) conceptualisation of rapport, positivity in an interviewing context included empathy, use of the suspect's name, politeness, humour, friendliness, and reassurance (Collins & Carthy, 2018). Attention included minimal encouragers (e.g., mmm, nodding), acknowledgements, paraphrasing, and identifying emotions. Coordination included agreement, credibility, information about process and procedure, and familiarisation with the room. Holmberg and Madsen (2014) also adapted Tickle-Degnan and Rosenthal's conceptualisation and included showing personal interest and creating a personal conversation in the attention component; showing positive attitude, friendliness, helpfulness, and empathy in the positivity component; and being cooperative and showing an obliging manner in the coordination component (Holmberg & Madsen, 2014).

In their study, Collins and Carthy (2018) found attention and coordination were the most commonly used components in investigative interviews. They also found that the use of these components was significantly correlated with an increase in the reporting of investigatively relevant information in interviews with males suspected of committingchild internet sex offences However, positivity was not correlated with an increase in the reporting of investigatively relevant information.

Rapport building in investigative interviews

Investigative interviewing has been described as "an attempt at social influence, with an interviewer attempting to gain the participation of, disclosure from, or admission from a source" (Abbe & Brandon, 2013, p. 242). In that context, rapport building is seen to facilitate relationship-based social influence. Given the sometimes adversarial nature of interviews with suspects, building rapport may be a challenging task (Abbe & Brandon, 2014). However, even in interviews with witnesses rapport building may be challenging due to, for example, witness reluctance, or the power differential between interviewer and interviewee. Generating a positive regard would be ideal, but respect will suffice, and would seem more likely in interviews with suspects (Abbe & Brandon, 2013). In investigative interviews, the parties are not necessarily "on the same page" and often the interviewer is asking for information that would be considered against the interest of the suspect. In the context of an investigative interview, it is imperative to avoid building pseudo-rapport. Gabbert and colleagues (2021) highlight this in their systematic review: "displaying signs of attentiveness without really listening, or over-using rapport behaviors, may quickly appear disingenuous or insincere" (p. 338).

Building rapport in investigative interviews can be further complicated by having a corroborator present (second interviewer). In their research examining rapport building in investigative interviews with one interviewer compared to two, Driskell and colleagues (2013) found there was no significant difference in interviewee rapport between interviews with two or three participants. Conducting interviews where an interpreter is present may also be seen as challenging for establishing and maintaining rapport. However, while some have thought this could reduce rapport, Walsh and colleagues (2020) found it was considered advantageous in that investigators indicated that interpreters' knowledge of the cultural considerations was helpful in building rapport.

Early investigative interviewing research focused on evaluating the effectiveness of the PEACE model and the impact of training on skills development (e.g., Clarke & Milne, 2001). As an evidence base was established, researchers moved to analysing the function of specific components within the model including, relevantly, rapport building. The difficulty of measuring the construct of rapport and its influence on an interview more generally is documented in the literature (Collins et al., 2002). In the context of an investigative interview, rapport building begins in the "Engage and explain" phase of the interview when the interviewer introduces themselves and provides instructions to the interviewee (Walsh & Bull, 2012). Rapport is further demonstrated in the "Account" phase of the interview by active listening, maintaining a calm persona, and speaking in a respectful tone (Walsh & Bull, 2012). The "Closure" phase also provides an obvious opportunity for demonstrating rapport. During this "Closure" phase the interviewer summarises the account and asks the interviewee if they would like to add or change anything, explains what will happen next, and tries to ensure that the interviewee is comfortable ending the interview—especially if another interview might need to be conducted later (Walsh & Bull, 2012).

In the context of the PEACE interview, a number of studies have examined rapport, although it has generally been limited to the "Engage and explain" phase. Their findings have been that not only inexperienced police officers, but also experienced police officers and benefit fraud investigators, performed the rapport component with an average score below PEACE standard (in interviews with witnesses and suspects, Clarke & Milne, 2001; Clarke et al., 2011; Dando et al., 2009a; Walsh & Bull, 2010a; Walsh & Milne, 2008). Reflecting the need to build and maintain rapport throughout the interview, Walsh and Bull (2012) examined the effect of rapport building and maintenance in the "Engage and explain", "Account", and "Closure" phases on interview outcomes with suspects of benefit fraud. When interviewer rapport was at a satisfactory or above level in the "Engage and explain" phase, the suspects subsequently provided three times as much relevant information compared to such rapport being below a satisfactory level. If rapport was maintained in the "Account" phase in such interviews, suspects provided five times as much information (the "Closure" phase overall was very often performed poorly). Collins and Carthy (2018) noted that positivity was mostly present in the beginning and end of interviews, whereas coordination occurred more frequently at the beginning and tapered off, but then remained consistent through the middle and end of the interview. Attention was found to be consistent throughout.

In considering the best approach for identifying vulnerability and tailoring the interview accordingly, it is essential that interviewers are able to observe and reflect as they conduct the interview. However, police officers have commented on the difficulty of combining listening and formulating a questioning strategy, with some police officers identifying aspects of self-reflection during the interview as contributing to the complexity (Griffiths et al., 2011). The ultimate aim for interviewers is to reflect within the interview and tailor an approach accordingly. However, their findings highlight the difficulty of reflecting and then implementing feedback while in the midst of conducting an interview.

Recent research examining police insight into rapport building in mock-interviews revealed that the "lead" interviewers' judgements of their rapport building with the suspect were less strongly correlated with the judgements of the other parties involved in the interview (the other "interviewer", suspect, and expert observer; Richardson & Nash, 2022), in comparison to the correlation between those parties. In the words of the authors: "the people leading these investigative interviews were uniquely poor at appraising the success of their own rapport-building" (Richardson & Nash, 2022, p. 39), possibly due to the additional demands placed on the lead interviewer limiting their ability to self-evaluate.

When examining the use of rapport building techniques by experienced practitioners across the world, the most commonly reported strategies were to identify and meet the basic needs of the interviewee, being patient, attempting to show kindness and respect, attempting to build a bond, and confronting the interviewee without insult (Sivasubramaniam & Goodman-Delahunty, 2021). In contrast, the least commonly used techniques were touching the interviewee in a friendly manner, and misrepresenting yourself by pretending to be from the interviewee's country or an ally of it (the sample was international). Finding common ground or shared experiences, or identities (e.g., as a parent), and allowing the interviewee to play the role of "teacher" were also utilised as strategies, although less frequently. In the same study, practitioners were asked how often they utilised particular techniques to control or alter the interview setting. The most common techniques were to attempt to reduce the interviewee's fear, offering genuine concern, appealing to the interviewee's self-interest, and appealing to the interviewee's conscience. Those less frequently reported were generally ones which could be contended as being coercive (e.g., offering moral rationalisations to enhance cooperation). These researchers found that many practitioners were aware of the importance of building rapport, and suggested that training can move from trying to convince investigators that rapport building is important to educating investigators about the use of persuasion and social influence in an interview context (Sivasubramaniam & Goodman-Delahunty, 2021).

Strategies for establishing rapport with vulnerable suspects

In examining the literature, there is clearly some consensus in terms of behaviours that are associated with rapport building. While there is no formula to follow (and the above described issues regarding pseudo-rapport are pertinent here) in their systematic review of rapport building in information gathering contexts, Gabbert and colleagues (2021) produced a database of rapport behaviours and categorised these as verbal, para-verbal, and non-verbal:

Verbal behaviours

- use of the interviewee's name;
- self-disclosure;
- showing personal interest;
- active listening;
- use of empathy.

Para-verbal behaviours

- tone of voice.

Non-verbal behaviours

- smiling;
- body-posture;
- eye contact;
- head-nodding.

They further analysed the behaviours according to their purpose: Personalising/relationship building

- personal interest/reciprocity;
- use of self-disclosure;
- use of interviewee's name.

Presenting an approachable demeanour

- tone of voice;
- smiling;
- open body language.

Paying attention

- active listening;
- head-nodding;
- empathic response.

Conclusion

Rapport building is built into the PEACE model of investigative interviewing, typically incorporated as part of the "Engage and explain" and "Account" phases. It is also recommended in the 2021 Mendez "Principles of Effective Interviewing".[1] Research has found that rapport building should occur throughout the interview, in what is called rapport maintenance. With respect to interviewing vulnerable suspects, rapport building is of particular importance as it increases the information elicited from the interviewee, and provides the opportunity to identify areas of vulnerability that may not be visible upon the suspect's initial presentation. Research has shown rapport building can be effectively trained, and results in a reduction in suspects' resistance to cooperation.

Note

1 Available at https://www.wcl.american.edu/impact/initiatives-programs/center/publications/documents/principles-on-effective-interviewing/

References

Abbe, A., & Brandon, S.E. (2013). The role of rapport in investigative interviewing: A review. *Journal of Investigative Psychology and Offender Profiling, 10*, 237–249. doi: 10.1002/jip.1386

Abbe, A., & Brandon, S.E. (2014). Building and maintaining rapport in investigative interviews. *Police Practice and Research, 15*(3), 207–220. doi: 10.1080/15614263.827835

Brimbal, L., Meissner, C.A., Kleinman, S.M., Phillips, E.L., Atkinson, D.J., Dianiska, R.E., ... & Jones, M.S. (2021). Evaluating the benefits of a rapport-based approach to investigative interviews: A training study with law enforcement investigators. *Law and Human Behavior, 45*(1), 55–67.

Collins, R., Lincoln, R., & Frank, M.G. (2002). The effect of rapport in forensic interviewing. *Psychiatry, Psychology and Law, 9,* 69–78.

Clarke, C., & Milne, B. (2001). *National evaluation of the PEACE investigative interviewing course (Police Research Award Scheme, Report No: PRAS/149).* Home Office.

Clarke, C., Milne, R., & Bull, R. (2011). Interviewing suspects of crime: The impact of PEACE training, supervision and the presence of a legal advisor. *Journal of Investigative Psychology and Offender Profiling, 8,* 149–162. doi: 10.1002/jip.144

Collins, K., & Carthy, N. (2018). No rapport, no comment: The relationship between rapport and communication during investigative interviews with suspects. *Journal of Investigative Psychology and Offender Profiling, 16,* 18–31. doi: 10.1002/jip.1517

Dando, C., Wilcock, R., & Milne, R. (2009). The cognitive interview: Novice police officers' witness/victim interviewing practices. *Psychology, Crime and Law, 15,* 679–696. doi: 10.1080/10683160802203963

Driskell, T., Blickensderfer, E.L., & Salas, E. (2013). Is three a crowd? Examining rapport in investigative interviews. *Group Dynamics: Theory, Research, and Practice, 17,* 1–13. doi: 10.1037/a0029686

Gabbert, F., Hope, L., Luther, K., Wright, G., Ng, M., & Oxburgh, G. (2021). Exploring the use of rapport in professional information-gathering contexts by systematically mapping the evidence base. *Applied Cognitive Psychology, 35,* 329–341. doi: 10.1002/acp.3762

Gilligan, C., Brubacher, S.P., & Powell, M.B. (2021). "We're all time poor": Experienced clinicians' and students' perception of challenges related to patient communication. *Teaching and Learning in Medicine, 34*(1), 1-12. doi: 10.1080/10401334.2021.1893175

Griffiths, A., Milne, B., & Cherryman, J. (2011). A question of control? The formulation of suspect and witness interview question strategies by advanced interviewers. *International Journal of Police Science and Management, 13,* 255–267.

Gudjonsson, G.H. (1994). Investigative interviewing: Recent developments and some fundamental issues. *International Review of Psychiatry, 6,* 237–245. doi: 10.3109/09540269409023262

Holmberg, U., & Madsen, K. (2014). Rapport operationalised as a humanitarian interview in investigative interview settings. *Psychiatry, Psychology and Law, 21,* 591–610. doi: 10.1080/13218719.2013.873975

Richardson, B.H., & Nash, R.A. (2022). 'Rapport myopia' in investigative interviews: Evidence from linguistic and subjective indicators of rapport. *Legal and Criminological Psychology, 27,* 32–47. doi: 10.1111/lcrp.12193

Sivasubramaniam, D., & Goodman-Delahunty, J. (2021). International consensus on effective and ineffective interviewing strategies: A survey of experienced practitioners. *Police Practice and Research, 22,* 921–937. doi: 10.1080/15614263.2019.1628756

Tickle-Degnen, M., & Rosenthal, R. (1990). The nature of rapport and its non-verbal correlates. *Psychological Inquiry, 1,* 285–293. Retrieved from: https://www-jstor-org.ezproxy.ecu.edu.au/stable/pdf/1449345.pdf?refreqid=excelsior%3A2c5653c67bfd6f82d1e2ddbf709f6582&ab_segments=&origin=

Walsh, D., & Bull, R. (2010). Interviewing suspects of fraud: An in-depth analysis of interviewing skills. *Journal of Psychiatry and Law, 38,* 99–135. Retrieved from http://heinonline.org

Walsh, D. & Bull, R. (2012). Examining rapport in investigative interviews with suspects: Does its building and maintenance work? *Journal of Police and Criminal Psychology, 27,* 73–84. doi: 10.1007/s11896-011-9087-x

Walsh, D., Oxburgh, G.E., & Amurun, T. (2020). Interpreter-assisted interviews: Examining investigators' and interpreters' views on their practice. *Journal of Police and Criminal Psychology, 35,* 318–327. doi: 10.1007/s11896-020-09366-2

Walsh, D.W., & Milne, R. (2008). Keeping the PEACE? A study of investigative interviewing practices in the public sector. *Legal and Criminological Psychology, 13,* 39–57. doi: 10.1348/135532506X157179

Chapter 3

Interviewing with a third party

Jane Tudor-Owen and Celine van Golde

Executive summary

The use of a third party (or parties) in an interview requires careful consideration as it is likely to alter the dynamic of the interview. Generally, a third party will be either an intermediary (e.g., Appropriate Adult or Interview Friend), lawyer, or interpreter. Each of these roles varies markedly and will therefore impact differently on the dynamic. This chapter will examine the role played by intermediaries, lawyers, and interpreters in the interview and offer guidelines with respect to conducting interviews where a third party is present.

Introduction

In interviews where a third party is present, there is an extra dimension to consider in both the planning and conducting of the interview. Third parties generally fall into one of three categories: intermediary, lawyer, or interpreter, but it is possible that an interview could have more than one additional (third) party aside from the suspect and police interviewers.

With respect to vulnerability, the presence of an intermediary or interpreter should be an indicator to police that additional consideration needs to be given to the particular circumstances of the suspect and what specific vulnerability might be present. Alternatively, it may be that police have insisted on the presence of either an intermediary or an interpreter in response to their own identification of a specific vulnerability to be addressed. In the latter circumstance, police are already alive to the issue.

The role of intermediaries, lawyers, and interpreters varies considerably. For example, an intermediary and lawyer may not say much at all in the course of an interview, whereas an interpreter facilitates the entirety of communication. To that end, the preparation required by the interviewer will understandably differ.

This chapter will examine the research concerning the use of third parties in interviews, then draw out the implications for investigative interviews with vulnerable suspects with respect to intermediaries, lawyers, and interpreters before providing some general guidelines that can be adopted across interview types.

Intermediaries

The *Police and Criminal Evidence Act 1984* enacted in England and Wales provides for the use of Appropriate Adults (AA) in interviews with vulnerable suspects. The role of an AA is to provide advice and support; however, little is known about the impact of an AA on the outcomes of interviews (Dehaghani, 2016; Farrugia & Gabbert, 2019), though research has found they typically say little (see below).

DOI: 10.4324/9781003145998-5

In contrast to what might have been anticipated by those drafting the guidance, research has found AAs are typically passive, and do not intervene as much as may have been anticipated. Medford and colleagues (2003) examined the use of AAs in interviews with juvenile and adult suspects and found that there were few verbal contributions from the AAs but there were other, more subtle impacts. For example, they found that: (i) there was less pressure from police in interviews where an AA was present and that the AA contributed more verbally when there was no legal representative present; (ii) it was more likely for adults to have a legal representative present in interviews where an AA was present and that the legal representative was more active in the interview.

More recent research has echoed the finding that AAs do not tend to contribute verbally. In their analysis of verbatim transcripts of interviews with 27 suspects with mental disorders, Farrugia and Gabbert (2019) found the AAs were significantly more likely to miss an opportunity than to intervene inappropriately according to official guidelines. In discussing non-interventions, Medford and colleagues (2003) highlighted that there had been opportunities to ensure the interview was conducted fairly (for example, prompting the advice of rights, caution, and challenging inappropriate interview tactics) but these had not been taken up by AAs.

Earlier, Medford and colleagues (2003) found that AAs made four times as many appropriate interventions than inappropriate. Such findings suggest AAs may not be aware of the opportunities at which they are able to intervene, or they may feel too intimidated to do so in an interview context. However, when they intervene it is most likely to be appropriate. Better training for AAs, as well as police interviewers, may assist with both of these potential issues. It is also important to determine what skills and competencies are necessary for effective AAs (P. Addison, personal communication, 12 December 2020).

Lawyers

In the context of an arrest, provisions are typically made to allow a suspect to obtain legal advice. Often this right is exercised using a telephone call; however, in a growing number of jurisdictions the suspect has the right to have a lawyer present during the interview with police. The extent to which this right is exercised varies; for example, it is more common to have a lawyer present in interviews in England than in Australia.

In 2007, Pearse and Gudjonsson found that in England, a legal advisor was present in 56% of interviews with suspects, and this advisor was a qualified solicitor in 24% of interviews (in the remaining 32% it was a legal representative). At the time, the authors noted that this was the highest proportion in research to date. Although Medford and colleagues (2003) did not find that the presence of an AA had an effect on the rate of admissions, they did find admissions were more likely when a legal representative was absent. In similar findings, Pearse and Gudjonsson found suspects less likely to confess and more likely to exercise their right to silence when a legal representative was present (2007).

The role of a lawyer in a police interview is determined, in part, by the timing of police disclosure to their client. That is, lawyers may well provide more fulsome advice to clients if they have already been made aware of the evidence against them (Sukumar et al., 2016b). Indeed, experimental research examining the advice given by criminal defence lawyers in England found that pre-interview disclosure of evidence allows lawyers to provide more comprehensive advice (Sukumar et al., 2016b). Further research conducted by Sukumar and colleagues (2016a) involving the researcher shadowing lawyers actually attending police stations found that when the police provided disclosure prior to the interview, this was more likely to be a summary of the evidence rather than allowing for inspection of it by the lawyer.

In these circumstances, there was a risk that the weight of the evidence could be exaggerated (Sukumar et al., 2016a), although in most cases lawyers were able to ask further questions of police. For police, the presence of a lawyer may restrict the use of interviewing techniques designed to elicit the truth; for example, following the strategic use of evidence (SUE) method of disclosure.

In Australia and several other countries, the right to legal advice is generally disclosed at the time of arrest and again at the outset of the interview (the latter may only be confirming the suspect has been afforded the right; it may not be a further invitation). However, anecdotal evidence suggests some interviewers will also inform the suspect at the beginning of the interview that they are able to stop the interview at any point for the purposes of seeking legal advice.

In addition to ensuring their clients understand their rights, lawyers can make further contributions in the course of an interview. Edwards and Stokoe (2011) examined the function of lawyers' contributions in interviews with suspects and noted their involvement in providing advice to clients during the course of the interview (ideally when police are not present), responding to invitations from police to add further information, and interjecting to clarify what police might be asking, or what they might be implying, during questioning.

Interpreters

In a world where travel and migration are usually frequent, notwithstanding the current restrictions as a result of COVID-19, there are increasing circumstances in investigative interviews where the interviewer and suspect are not sufficiently fluent in a common language, resulting in difficulties engaging and communicating (Ewens et al., 2016). In Chapter 11 of this book, we will discuss specific considerations for conducting interviews with Culturally and Linguistically Diverse populations. In that chapter, we will discuss how to identify whether the suspect requires an interpreter. At times, the decision to engage an interpreter in the interests of fairness to the suspect will be an easy one; however, at other times it will be less so, particularly if the suspect is unwilling due to the small size of the population and the risk of confidentiality being compromised as a result of knowing the interpreter personally.

Conducting an interview with an interpreter present is both time consuming and complex. This complexity is further enhanced when considering the nature of an interview with a suspect who is likely to be anxious. Given the use of particular strategies to increase cognitive load in interviews with suspects (see e.g., Vrij et al., 2008), it is important to consider the additional layer of communicating through an interpreter. For the interpreter, in addition to the requirement of being able to translate from one language to another, there is also the added pressure of the environment. Police officers utilising interpreting services must be cognisant of these factors.

In terms of individual strategies, Ewens and colleagues (2016) examined whether it was possible to use instructions to recall an event in reverse order. This was used as a method by which to detect deception in mock-interviews where the participant either communicated using English where their English was not fluent or utilised an interpreter. Their findings revealed that it was possible to differentiate between participants lying and participants telling the truth when an interpreter was used, but there was no significant difference between the groups when the participant was communicating in English. The authors suggested that the cognitive loading of both recalling an account in reverse order and engaging with an interpreter was too high to detect differences.

In contrast, research conducted by Vrij and Leal (2020) found that complication proportions could be used to differentiate between truth tellers and liars in interviews where an interpreter was present. They note that in interviews with interpreters, interviewees in general were less likely to reveal complications (non-essential aspects of an account), self-handicapping strategies (justifications for why information is limited), and common knowledge details. However, they were still able to differentiate between truth tellers and liars using relevant calculations of these. One explanation for less complications, self-handicapping strategies, and common knowledge details (or details in general) is that interviewees are concerned about being efficient given the prolonged nature of interviews where an interpreter is present, or that the interpreter does not translate these details (Vrij & Leal, 2020; Vrij et al., 2018).

Strategies for interviewing with third parties

While each circumstance will be different, there are some general principles to follow when conducting interviews that include a third party (intermediary, lawyer, or interpreter). In brief, preparation is key:

- Where possible, have a discussion with the third party/parties prior to the interview so you can explain your expectations and address any questions they might have. Depending on the circumstances, it may be appropriate to have this discussion once the recording of the interview has begun.
- Consider logistics. Is the interview room big enough to accommodate all parties comfortably while maintaining recording integrity (sound and visual)?
- Speak slowly and clearly.
- Address the suspect (unless you have something to direct to the third party specifically). This direction can be difficult to follow when there is an interpreter present, as they will be conveying the information, but make sure you are directing your questions to the suspect and observing their body language for any additional cues.

Conclusion

Intermediaries, lawyers, and interpreters serve an important function in minimising the risks for vulnerable suspects and providing the opportunity for police to elicit information in accordance with rules requiring fairness and voluntariness in police interviews. However, in order for these third parties to perform their function, it is imperative they are aware of the scope of their role and act accordingly.

Having a third party present in an interview does not, in and of itself, lead to particular outcomes. Rather, the nature of the third party's role may have a particular influence. For example, the use of an interpreter usually increases the understanding of the suspect and interviewer with respect to what is being communicated, whereas the presence of a lawyer is more likely to impact the extent to which the suspect communicates at all, as well as the likelihood of a confession. Current research suggests the presence of an Appropriate Adult is unlikely to have significant influence until there is more clarity for Appropriate Adults about their role in an interview.

Having additional parties in an interview requires careful planning to minimise unexpected influences. Research suggests that having an Appropriate Adult, lawyer, and/or interpreter present is likely to change the dynamic, and interviewers need to be cognisant of the potential impact, emphasising the need for preparation and planning.

References

Dehaghani, R. (2016). He's just not that vulnerable: Exploring the implementation of the Appropriate Adult safeguard in police custody. *The Howard Journal of Crime and Justice, 55*, 396–413. Doi: 10.1111/hojo.12178

Edwards, D., & Stokoe, E. (2011). "You don't have to answer": Lawyers' contributions in police interrogations of suspects. *Research of Language and Social Interaction, 44*, 21–43. Doi: 10.1080/08351813.2011.543877

Ewens, S., Vrij, A., Mann, S., & Leal, S. (2016). Using the reverse order techniques with non-native speakers or through an interpreter. *Applied Cognitive Psychology, 30*, 242–249. Doi: 10.1002/acp.3196

Farrugia, L., & Gabbert, F. (2019). The "appropriate adult": What they do and what they should do in police interviews with mentally disordered suspects. *Criminal Behaviour and Mental Health, 29*, 134–141. Doi: 10.1002/cbm.2111

Medford, S., Gudjonsson, G.H., & Pearse, J. (2003). The efficacy of the appropriate adult safeguard during police interviewing. *Legal and Criminological Psychology, 8*, 253–266.

Pearse, J., & Gudjonsson, G. (1997). Police interviewing and legal representation: A field study. *Journal of Forensic Psychiatry, 8*, 200–208. Doi: 10.1080/09585189708412005

Sukumar, D., Hodgson, J.S., & Wade, K.A. (2016a). Behind closed doors: Live observations of current police station disclosure practices and lawyer-client consultations. *Criminal Law Review, 12*, 900–914.

Sukumar, D., Hodgson, J.S., & Wade, K.A. (2016b). How the timing of police evidence disclosure impacts custodial legal advice. *The International Journal of Evidence & Proof, 20*, 200–216. Doi: 10.1177/1365712716643548

Vrij, A., & Leal, S. (2020). Proportion of complication in interpreter-absent and interpreter-present interviews. *Psychiatry, Psychology and Law, 27*, 155–164. Doi: 10.1080/13218719.2019.1705197

Vrij, A., Leal, S., Mann, S., Fisher, R.P., Dalton, G., Jo, E., Shaboltas, A., Khaleeva, M., Granskaya, J., & Houston, K. (2018). Using unexpected questions to elicit information and cues to deceit in interpreter-based interviews. *Applied Cognitive Psychology, 32*, 94–104. Doi: 10.1002/acp.3382

Vrij, A., Mann, S.A., Fisher, R.P., Leal, S., Milne, R., & Bull, R. (2008). Increasing cognitive load to facilitate lie detection: The benefit of recalling an event in reverse order. *Law and Human Behavior, 32*(3), 253–265.

Chapter 4

Training interviewers

Ray Bull and Becky Milne

Executive summary

At the point at which it is established that a particular course of action is required, attention necessarily turns to the "how" in making it happen. Interview training has been the subject of extensive research both before and after the introduction of the PEACE model. In this chapter, we examine the impact of training on interview performance, and the key principles required to effect sustained change in interviewing practice. Although the purpose is to inform training police in how to interview vulnerable suspects, the principles and guidance can be applied to any form of interviewing.

Introduction

Of the "around 1 million" police interviews with adult suspects over a 12-month period to 2019 in England and Wales, approximately 17% (i.e., 17,000) involved vulnerable persons (as defined in official documents).[1] In the Netherlands, Geijsen, de Ruiter, and Kop (2018) found in their first study that of those whose assessments were completed about 60% were found to have mental health issues, a significant proportionconsidering it is just one type of vulnerability relevant to conducting investigative interviews with suspects. A consideration of relevance to training is that, to an extent, all suspects are vulnerable (Dehaghani, 2020). Whereas some may be particularly vulnerable because of factors they bring to interviews, others become vulnerable due to the situation (for example, being suspected of a crime and/or the nature/skill of the interviewing), an idea explored in detail in Chapter 1.

Even though the proportion of suspects who are deemed to be vulnerable is high, Gulati, Cusack, Kelly, Kilcommins, and Dunne (2020) noted that "the most striking finding from our systematic review is the paucity of published studies that include a qualitative description of the experiences of" suspects with intellectual disabilities in their interactions with law enforcement (p. 5). They also noted that the themes which arose "emphasise the importance of having specialist interviewers who can better undertake interviews with suspects with intellectual disabilities" (p. 5), further emphasising the importance of training. In their recent article on protecting vulnerable suspects in police investigations Mergaerts and Dehaghani (2020) stated that "The jurisdiction of England and Wales has had a long tradition of protecting vulnerable suspects" (p. 318) and that the relevant "Codes of Practice" document "urges officers to take special care when questioning vulnerable suspects" (p. 322). However, it is important to note at the outset that the "Codes" actually say rather little about how best to question/interview.

DOI: 10.4324/9781003145998-6

In 2020 the Home Office in England and Wales published its updated and wide-ranging guidance document entitled "Interviewing suspects".[2] Among its 64 pages were relatively few on actual interviewing and even fewer on "Interviewing juveniles and the vulnerable". These pages very briefly outlined the five phases of the PEACE interview model, stating "When you plan an interview with a suspect you must follow the model" (p. 27) and "You must always take special care when you question juveniles, the mentally disordered or otherwise mentally vulnerable people" (p. 50). Although this official document itself provided very little guidance on conducting interviews with vulnerable suspects, it provided clear instruction on the interviewing framework that "must" be followed, this being the PEACE model/method.

The PEACE model

Draft reports of research studies conducted soon after the tape-recording of interviews with suspects in England became mandatory in 1986 led the government and police chiefs' association to set up (in 1991) a working party of experienced police investigators to develop up-to-date training on interviewing. They recommended what they called the PEACE model. This change began in 1992 and involved guidance documents and training courses that police interviewers in England and Wales must attend and contained much research-based findings from psychology (Milne & Bull, 1999). In 1990, during the time in which these detectives were having their working party meetings, senior police officer, Tom Williamson, convened a different small working party of detectives and psychologists (including Eric Shepherd, Stephen Moston, and Ray Bull). In 1991 that group produced an (unpublished) review of notions from psychology that would be useful in improving interviewing. This was given to the national team of detectives that was developing PEACE who in turn adopted much of its contents.

PEACE is an acronym for Planning and preparation; Engage and explain; Account, clarification, and challenge; Closure; and Evaluation. An outline of the PEACE method was provided in an Australian Institute of Criminology document entitled "Police interviews with vulnerable adult suspects" (Bartels, 2011) that focussed not directly on interviewing strategies but on the relevant legislation and policies in different parts of the country for which there was "a wide disparity" (p. 7). Bartels noted there should be compliance "with Australia's requirements under the *Convention on the Rights of Persons with Disabilities* to 'promote appropriate training for … police and prison staff' (Article 13)" (p. 11). Also in Australia, Herrington and Roberts (2012) noted that "Little work has been done on how to interview suspects with a PV" (i.e., a psychological vulnerability) and that "The PEACE method of investigative interviewing provides a useful structure for these interviews" (p. 183). In 2018 the Council of Europe published "A brief introduction to investigative interviewing: A practitioner's guide" that provides an overview of the PEACE method. In England and Wales the College of Policing has made guidance on investigative interviewing/the PEACE method publicly available.[3] Farrugia and Gabbert (2020b) noted that although official guidance to police in England and Wales on the interviewing of vulnerable suspects (referred to as "Code C") mentions that special care be taken, this particular guidance does not provide detail on how to do this. Another official guidance document does provide extensive information on how to interview vulnerable people, but this was designed for victims/witnesses (i.e., "Achieving best evidence in criminal proceedings: Guidance on interviewing victims and witnesses, and on using special measures"). Of course, partly because some suspects can also be witnesses, the guidance provided by Achieving Best Evidence (ABE; 2022) can be of relevance when interviewing them.

Research on interviewing skills

Having established the PEACE model as the most appropriate model for interviewing vulnerable suspects, it is pertinent to turn attention to research examining interviewing skills in interviews with vulnerable suspects. In their analyses of police interviews with suspects who had "mental health disorders" (p. 20) compared to suspects without this vulnerability, Farrugia and Gabbert (2022) found no differences regarding the rates of interviewers asking various question types between the two groups of suspects (except for "echo questions" in which the interviewers echo what the suspect has just communicated), such a finding implying that the mental health disorders had little effect on the interviewing. The vulnerable suspects more frequently sought clarification of the questions being put to them especially for open questions and whereas the interviewers more often used the language "to suit the abilities and understanding of suspects with mental health disorders" (p. 25), they also more often used "poor interview techniques such as minimisation … with the vulnerable suspects" (p. 25).[4]

In the Netherlands, Geijsen et al. (2018a) found in their second study that, despite the prevalence of vulnerabilities found in their first study, half of approximately 100 experienced police interviewers said that they had not interviewed a vulnerable suspect in the previous year, and half indicated that they took no special precautions when interviewing vulnerable suspects. Further, around 75% of these interviewers said they had not received specialised interview training. In another Dutch study, suspects in police custody were psychologically screened for intellectual disabilities, mental disorders, abnormal mental states, and substance abuse (Geijsen et al., 2018). They found 69% of the suspects could be deemed vulnerable, yet most of them were, in the opinion of the researchers, interviewed inappropriately. During the time that the data were being gathered in these two studies the Dutch police commenced a series of training for interviewing vulnerable suspects in the more serious cases and, at the time of writing, over 220 detectives have received such training.[5]

What training should include

As previously discussed, in England and Wales extensive guidance regarding the investigative interviewing of vulnerable people has been made available by the government and the national College of Policing.[6] Even though such guidance was written with regard to vulnerable witnesses and victims, much of it is of direct relevance to the interviewing of vulnerable suspects and therefore to training (and supervising).

The extensive information provided by the National College of Policing mirrors that in the ABE, the contents of which are research- and evidence-based. In the present chapter on training, there is only space to provide an overview of aspects of such documents relevant to interviewing vulnerable suspects. Bevan (2017) noted that

> the approach to be taken when interviewing vulnerable suspects is not set out in detailed guidance in the same way as the approach required when interviewing a child or vulnerable adult as a witness. Nonetheless, … principles … guidance for the questioning of vulnerable witnesses and victims are applicable to the investigative interviewers of vulnerable suspects.
>
> (p. 129)

The "phased approach"

The interviewing guidance provided by the PEACE method and by ABE are strikingly similar (largely because they are both based on or are in line with relevant research). The major section on interviewing vulnerable people in the 2002 ABE (that Ray Bull drafted for government) and the PEACE method both strongly recommended a *"phased approach"* involving:

1. Establish rapport.
2. Free narrative recall.
3. Questioning (in the hierarchy of):
   open questions;
   specific questions;
   closed questions;
   leading questions (only when necessary).
4. Closure: recapitulation and ensuring the interviewee leaves in a positive frame of mind. Regarding this approach, ABE asserts that "The sound legal framework it provides should not be departed from by interviewers unless they have discussed and agreed the reasons for doing so with their senior manager(s)" (2022, p. 76).

Planning

ABE notes the crucial importance of planning: "A well-conducted interview will only occur if appropriate planning has taken place" (2022, p. 17). The planning for each interview should provide guidance to the interviewer about what might be achieved in each of the four main phases of the interview (e.g., "Is this vulnerable person likely to able to communicate via free narrative?").

One skill fundamental to the interviewing of any person is the conducting of effective planning and preparation (also considered in Chapter 2). Both experienced professionals and relevant researchers have repeatedly emphasised that this is the most fundamental and crucial of all interviewing skills. Although what an interviewer actually does during an interview is of great importance, good planning and preparation are even more important, especially with vulnerable interviewees. It is more cost-effective to devote time to proper planning and preparation than to conduct an interview in an ill-prepared and ill-planned way.

A considerable proportion of vulnerable suspects will require that their interviews go at a slow pace. This is because many of them, due to their current state/condition and the situation, will have a slower rate of understanding, thinking, and replying than people without specific vulnerabilities. Both research and best practice have found that interviewers will need to be prepared to:

- slow down their speech rate;
- allow extra time for the interviewee to take in what has just been said;
- provide time for the interviewee to prepare a response;
- be patient if the suspect replies slowly;
- avoid immediately posing the next question;
- avoid interrupting.

The rapport phase (called "Engage and explain" in the PEACE method)

It is crucial to be aware that a vulnerable suspect is likely to provide more information and detail relevant to the investigation if the interviewer is able to succeed in establishing good rapport. Indeed, ABE stresses that rapport is an essential part of the interview (2022). A comprehensive overview of research and good practice in many jurisdictions has found strong agreement that establishing and maintaining rapport is of the utmost importance (Bull, 2013; Walsh & Bull, 2012). With regard to the interviewing of suspects with a mental disorder, Oxburgh, Gabbert, Milne, and Cherryman (2016) found police interviewers to report a positive relationship between rapport and amount of information gained. Demonstrating rapport, enhanced by appropriate empathy and good listening skills, is very important (Baker-Eck, Bull, & Walsh, 2020; Bull & Baker-Eck, 2020).

In this phase, it should be conveyed to the interviewee that if the interviewer asks a question that the vulnerable person does not know the answer to, the interviewer would be happy for them to indicate, "I don't know". People may be unwilling to admit "I don't know" unless they are assisted to realise it is the preferred response if that is the case. While this is the appropriate course of action in all interviews, in interviews with vulnerable suspects, and particularly those who may be more suggestible, this is important to emphasise. One strategy to ensure the suspect understands is to pose questions to them. For example, "If I ask you ten questions, how many questions do you have to answer?" and "If I ask you something you don't know the answer to, what should you say?" Having these safeguards in place further emphasises commitment to fairness and voluntariness, the cornerstone of admissibility.

The "free narrative" phase follows on from the rapport phase. Having established rapport, if it is deemed appropriate to continue with the interview, then the suspect should be asked to provide an account of the events in their own words. Only the most general, open-ended prompts should be used as guidance in this phase. If the suspect does respond to such prompts, then the interviewer can encourage them to give a free narrative account of events in their own words without interruptions from the interviewer. During this phase, the interviewer's role is to act as a facilitator, not an interrogator. A proportion of vulnerable suspects may be unable to provide free narrative accounts but may be able to respond to skilled questioning. In those circumstances, always make an initial attempt to elicit a free recall narrative before beginning questioning.

Questioning

Research findings have consistently shown that improper questioning of suspects is a greater source of distortion of their accounts than their memory issues. ABE noted that during the free narrative phase of an interview most interviewees will not be able to recall everything relevant that is in their memory and that "most witnesses will not be able to recall everything relevant that is in their memory. Therefore, their accounts could greatly benefit from the interviewer asking appropriate questions that assist further recall" (2022, p. 207).

Both research and best practice have found that vulnerable interviewees may well have great difficulty with questions unless these are simple, do not contain jargon, do not contain abstract words and/or abstract ideas, contain only one point per question, are not too directive/suggestive, and do not contain double negatives.

Best practice recommends that the questioning phase commences with open questions prior to closed questions because the former usually produce better information than the latter; however, open questions may not be the most appropriate for some vulnerable people (Bearman, Brubacher, Timms, & Powell, 2019). For example, using a mock theft paradigm Farrugia and Gabbert (2022) found that undergraduate participants (suspects) who had "mental health conditions" provided investigation-relevant information equally well whether the questions put to them were open or closed, whereas the participants without "mental health conditions" performed better in response to open questions. However, to be a skilled interviewer requires the ability to be able to effectively distinguish between the various types of questions and to compose examples of each type—skills that not all interviewers possess (Yii, Powell, & Guadagno, 2014). In circumstances where one size does not fit all, it also requires skills in determining which approach fits the circumstances and adapting accordingly.

When a suspect provides information that contradicts information known to the interviewer, this would normally result in the interviewer asking a question. When to disclose such information to a suspect is beyond the scope of the present chapter (see Bull, 2014; Sandham, Dando, Bull, & Ormerod, 2020). However, we should mention here that O'Mahony et al. (2012) noted that for vulnerable suspects "the evidence base for appropriate questioning styles ... is limited" (p. 301) and that it is especially difficult to challenge discrepancies in a vulnerable suspect's account. They concluded that research and development have "yet to focus ... on whether investigators can adequately fulfil their role in challenging the account of a vulnerable suspect" (p. 310). In the years since 2012 little progress has been made on this point that remains a matter for trainers, management, and supervisors to develop policy on. Central to any developments in challenging vulnerable suspects is upholding the principles of fairness and voluntariness, something even more complicated and nuanced when interviewing vulnerable suspects.

Because vulnerable suspects will experience difficulty if the interviewer "topic hops" when questioning them, ABE states that

> the interviewer should subdivide the witness's account into manageable topics or episodes and seek elaboration on each area using open-ended and then specific-closed questions. Each topic or episode should be systematically dealt with until the witness is unable to provide any more information. Interviewers can also summarise what the witness has said, using their own words, in relation to each topic or episode.
>
> (2022, p. 207)

To assist the interviewee (for present purposes, the suspect), the interviewer should adopt the practice of signposting. For example, indicating a change of topic by saying, for example, "I'd now like to ask you about something else".

In all contexts, interviewers need to be aware of the common human frailty of ignoring information contrary to one's own view. Research on interviewing has repeatedly found that interviewers ignore information that does not fit with their assumptions. This ignoring of "unwanted" information may be even more likely to affect interviewers of vulnerable people if they believe such interviewees to be less competent than ordinary people. Thus, one important role for any "accompanying interviewer" is to check that the "lead interviewer" does not ignore information provided by the suspect that differs from what the interviewer may be expecting.

The "Closure" phase

"Closure" is the fourth major phase of the interview and has two major parts, these being recapitulation and closure. This phase should normally include the following:

1. Check with the accompanying interviewer (if there is one).
2. Summarise the evidentially important information provided by the suspect.
3. Invite and answer any questions from the suspect.
4. Thank the suspect for their time and effort.
5. Identify the next steps in the process.
6. Return to rapport/neutral topics.

United Nations guidance

In 2016, the United Nations (UN) produced the "Special Rapporteur on torture and other cruel, inhuman or degrading treatment or punishment" that was transmitted by the UN Secretary-General to the UN General Assembly. The Special Rapporteur stated that

> The protocol must design a model that is non-coercive, ethically sound, evidence-based and research-based and empirically founded. It should champion a culture of human rights compliance, A/71/298 8/25 16-13568 the highest standards of professionalism and the use of fair and ethical practices that demonstrably enhance the effectiveness of interviews and the elicitation of accurate and reliable information.
>
> (p. 7)

In 2020, the views of professionals who had extensive experience of interviewing people with communication impairments in forensic contexts indicated that they expressed widespread support for the type of interviewing approach outlined above (Bearman, Earhart, Timms, & Powell, 2020). The training of the interviewers of vulnerable people should emphasise that many such people have developed a variety of life skills appropriate to their circumstances and that some of these skills could be relevant to interviewing/communicating. As stated by Haben Girma in her 2019 book entitled *The Deafblind Woman Who Conquered Harvard Law*: "Some-day the world will learn that people with disabilities are talented, too" (p. 171).

Further consideration will be needed to develop training for situations in which the training cannot be conducted face-to-face (such as in countries with wide geographical dispersion of people/professionals or in unusual circumstances such as the COVID-19 pandemic of 2020). As yet, it seems that procedures for achieving this regarding the interviewing of vulnerable suspects have not been developed. However, at least one system has been developed regarding the forensic interviewing of children (see Benson and Powell, 2015; Powell, Guadagno, & Benson, 2016).

The presence at interviews of advisors

Chapter 3 contains a discussion of third parties in interviews with vulnerable suspects; however, in this chapter it is important to consider implications for training specifically. Training should alert trainees to be aware that the presence of a defence lawyer/legal advisor or another adult (such as a child's parent or Appropriate Adult) should not unduly influence their interviewing. On the one hand, a parent or legal advisor may say nothing during an interview, but on the other hand they may intervene. Regarding those who are present but saying nothing, Mindthoff, Malloy, and Hohs (2020) asked members of the public to read summaries of the trial of a 15-year-old male defendant that included a description of the police interview with him. Some read the summary in which either a defence lawyer or the adolescent's parent was present at the interview (but who remained quiet). Higher conviction rates occurred when either of these adults had been present compared to when they were not present (in one of the two studies). In their second study, the presence of a defence lawyer during the police interview was associated with the public's more positive views of the interviewing and less concern about the adolescent's vulnerability. In one criminal case in which Ray Bull was asked to provide an expert opinion on the police interviewing of a young boy suspected of raping a young girl, during the interview the boy's father on several occasions prompted his son to admit to the crime. These examples highlight the way in which the presence (or absence) of third parties can influence the actions of people within the interview as well as perceptions of the interview, or interview parties. As such, it is important to be mindful about any impact third parties may have, and to mitigate this where possible; for example, by meeting with third parties prior to interviews and explaining their role. This could also be undertaken while the interview is being recorded for the benefit of a jury viewing it at a later date. Please see Chapter 3 for more detail regarding interviews with third parties.

Soon after the European Union ruling that all member countries should have legislation enabling a legal advisor to be present at the interviews with suspects (Mergaerts, Van Daele, & Vervaeke, 2018), Ray Bull and Gary Shaw, the Police National Advisor on the interviewing of suspects in England and Wales, were invited to a European country to discuss this new situation with police. The police (in several European countries) had raised concerns about this new legislation and Gary Shaw was asked to describe any relevant problems experienced in his country (where extensive training on the interviewing of suspects had been in place since 1992—the PEACE method). In reply, Gary (supported by Ray) made the crucial point that interventions by defence lawyers (who receive training on when to intervene in the interviews) were relatively rare, this being attributable to the positive qualities of the interviewing.

Does the interviewing style really matter?

A growing number of studies have examined the relationship between interviewing style and suspects' behaviour. The pioneering 2002 study by Holmberg and Christianson found that fewer convicted persons reported having confessed when interviewed/interrogated in a "dominant" style than those interviewed in a "humane" style. In Japan, a study by Wachi, Watanabe, Yokota, Otsuka, and Lamb (2016) produced a similar finding. (Also see Bull, 2019; Bull & Rachlew, 2019; Leahy-Harland & Bull, 2017.) In Canada, Barron (2017) compared the real-life interviews with suspects of PEACE-trained and "untrained" police, finding that the former group used more open questions and fewer leading questions but fewer facilitators. The suspects in the former group "provided significantly greater amounts of information" (p. 11) though no difference in court outcomes was found.

In 2020 Brimbal, Bradford, Jackson, Hartwig, and Joseph considered issues relevant to police officers' adopting research-based interviewing methods. They noted that it had been suggested that police officers' compliance with (especially new) regulations/rules/guidance might be enhanced if their supervisors adhere to principles of procedural justice (i.e., the degree to which people perceive those in authority apply processes/make decisions about them in a fair and just way). In their own research they found that police investigators who believed their supervisors behaved in line with procedural justice identified to a greater extent with their organisation. Procedural justice was also found to be related to openness to change. The most important factor that predicted officers' future use of the evidence-based training they had been trained in (involving topics such as rapport, empathy, respect, understanding) was motivation to attend such training—hence an important role for supervisors and managers.

Conclusion

At the outset of this chapter it was established that every person interviewed by police is vulnerable, to a greater or lesser extent. Looking around the world, there is limited formal guidance available, with the exception of guidelines pertaining to interviewing children specifically. There appears to be an awareness of the need to tread carefully in interviews with people deemed vulnerable, but limited instruction available. In this chapter, the PEACE model of interviewing was outlined, highlighting the similarity of the phases of the model with what is recommended in the ABE protocol, revised in 2022 for interviews with children. It is suggested, therefore, that training interviewers to interview vulnerable people should consider the application of the principles outlined in ABE, in combination with those pertaining to the PEACE model in order to best safeguard the process. Given we have established that all suspects bear some vulnerability, it is imperative that all police are provided with training to facilitate interviews with vulnerable people.

Notes

1 Information provided by the UK national newspaper *The Guardian* in 2019 (see https://www.theguardian.com/uk-news/2019/may/31/report-raises-alarm-over-police-detention-of-vulnerable-suspects-national-appropriate-adult-network).
2 Available at https://www.gov.uk/government/publications/interviewing-suspects.
3 https://www.app.college.police.uk/app-content/investigations/investigative-interviewing/.
4 Though the actual operational definition of minimisation used in this publication was not provided.
5 Personal communication from Martijn Van Beek of the Dutch national police academy.
6 https://www.cps.gov.uk/sites/default/files/documents/legal_guidance/best_evidence_in_criminal_proceedings.pdf; https://www.whatdotheyknow.com/request/366866/response/900021/attach/8/Specialist%20Investigative%20Interviewing%20Vulnerable%20Adult%20Witness%20Interview.pdf; also see Bull, 1995; Milne & Bull, 1999.

References

Baker-Eck, B., Bull, R., & Walsh, D. (In press). Investigative empathy: Five types of cognitive empathy in a field study of investigative interviews with suspects of sexual offences. *Investigative Interviewing: Research and Practice*.

Barron, W.T. (2017). *The 'PEACE' model of investigative interviewing: A comparison of trained and untrained suspect interviewers* [Master dissertation, Memorial University of Newfoundland].

Bartels, L. (2011). *Police interviews with vulnerable adult suspects: Report no. 21*. Australian Institute of Criminology.

Bearman, M., Brubacher, S.P., Timms, L., & Powell, M. (2019). Trial of three investigative interview techniques with minimally verbal adults reporting about occurrences of a staged repeated event. *Psychology, Public Policy, and Law, 25*(4), 239.

Bearman, M., Earhart, B., Timms, L., & Powell, M. (2021). Professionals' views on how to conduct investigative interviews with adults with limited expressive language. *Psychiatry, Psychology and Law, 38*, 104–119.

Benson, M., & Powell, M. (2015). Evaluation of a comprehensive interactive training system for investigative interviewers of children. *Psychology, Public Policy, and Law, 21*(3), 309–322.

Bevan, M. (2017). Vulnerable suspects: The investigation stage. In Cooper, P. & Norton, H. (Eds.), *Vulnerable people and the criminal justice system: A guide to law and practice* (pp. 95–138). Oxford University Press.

Bull, R. (1995). Interviewing people with communication disabilities. In R. Bull & D. Carson (Eds.), *Handbook of psychology in legal contexts*. Wiley.

Bull, R. (2014). When in interviews to disclose information to suspects and to challenge them? In R. Bull (Ed.), *Investigative interviewing*. Springer.

Bull, R. (2019). Roar or PEACE: Is it a tall story? In R. Bull & I. Blandon-Gitlin (Eds.), *Routledge International handbook of legal and investigative psychology*. Routledge.

Bull, R., & Baker-Eck, B. (2020). Obtaining from suspects valid discourse 'PEACE'-fully: What role for rapport and empathy? In M. Mason and F. Rock (Eds.), *The discourse of police interviews*. University of Chicago Press.

Bull, R., & Rachlew, A. (2019). Investigative interviewing: From England to Norway and beyond. In S. Barela, M. Fallon, G. Gaggioli, & J. Ohlin (Eds.), *Interrogation and torture: Research on efficacy, and its integration with morality and legality*. Oxford University Press.

Council of Europe. (2018). *A brief introduction to investigative interviewing: A practitioner's guide*. Council of Europe.

Dehaghani, R. (2020). Interrogating vulnerability: Reframing the vulnerable suspect in police custody. *Social & Legal Studies*. doi: 10.1177/0964663920921921

Farrugia, L., & Gabbert, F. (2022). Forensic interviewing of mentally disordered suspects: The impact of interview style on investigation outcomes. *Current Psychology, 41,* 3216–3224.

Farrugia, L., & Gabbert, F. (2020). Vulnerable suspects in police interviews: Exploring current practice in England and Wales. *Journal of Investigative Psychology and Offender Profiling, 17*(1), 17–30.

Geijsen, K., Vanbelle, S., Kop, N., and de Ruiter, C. (2018). The interrogation of vulnerable suspects in the Netherlands: An exploratory study. *Investigative Interviewing: Research and Practice, 9*(1), 59–97.

Girma, H. (2019). *Haben: The deafblind woman who conquered harvard law.* Twelve.

Gulati, G., Cusack, A., Kelly, B.D., Kilcommins, S., & Dunne, C.P. (2020). Experiences of people with intellectual disabilities encountering law enforcement officials as the suspects of crime: A narrative systematic review. *International Journal of Law and Psychiatry, 71,* 101609.

Herrington, V., & Roberts, K. (2012). Addressing psychological vulnerability in the police suspect interview. *Policing: A Journal of Policy and Practice, 6*(2), 177–186.

Leahy-Harland, S., & Bull, R. (2017). Police strategies and suspect responses in real-life serious crime interviews. *Journal of Police and Criminal Psychology, 32,* 138–151.

Mergaerts, L., & Dehaghani, R. (2020). Protecting vulnerable suspects in police investigations in Europe: Lessons learned from England and Wales and Belgium. *New Journal of European Criminal Law, 11*(3), 313–334.

Mergaerts, L., Van Daele, D., & Vervaeke, G. (2018). Challenges in defining and identifying a suspect's vulnerability in criminal proceedings: What's in a name and who's to blame?. In P. Cooper and L. Hunting (Eds.), *Access to Justice for Vulnerable People* (pp. 49–53). Wildy.

Mindthoff, A., Malloy, L.C., & Höhs, J.M. (2020). Mock jurors' perceptions and case decisions following a juvenile interrogation: Investigating the roles of interested adults and confession type. *Law and Human Behavior, 44*(3), 209–222.

O'Mahony, B.M., Milne, B., & Grant, T. (2012). To challenge, or not to challenge? Best practice when interviewing vulnerable suspects. *Policing: A Journal of Policy and Practice, 6*(3), 301–313.

Oxburgh, L., Gabbert, F., Milne, R., & Cherryman, J. (2016). Police officers' perceptions and experiences with mentally disordered suspects. *International Journal of Law and Psychiatry, 49,* 138–146.

Powell, M., Guadagno, B., & Benson, M. (2016). Improving child investigative interviewer performance through computer-based learning activities. *Policing and Society, 26*(4), 365–374.

Sandham, A., Dando, C., Bull, R., & Ormerod, T. (2022). Improving professional observers' veracity judgements by tactical interviewing. *Journal of Police and Criminal Psychology, 37,* 279–287.

Wachi, T., Watanabe, K., Yokota, K., Otsuka, Y., & Lamb, M.E. (2016). Japanese suspect interviews, confessions, and related factors. *Journal of Police and Criminal Psychology, 31*(3), 217–227.

Walsh, D., & Bull, R. (2012). Examining rapport in investigative interviews with suspects: Does its building and maintenance work? *Journal of Police and Criminal Psychology, 27,* 73–84.

Yii, S.L.B., Powell, M.B., & Guadagno, B. (2014). The association between investigative interviewers' knowledge of question type and adherence to best practice interviewing. *Legal and Criminological Psychology, 19*(2), 270–281.

Chapter 5

Interview supervision and management

Ray Bull and Becky Milne

Executive summary

Research has shown that there is sometimes a gap between how a person perceives their performance and an objective assessment of that performance by another party. This chapter discusses the role of supervision and training in assisting police to more accurately evaluate their own performance and ultimately increase their interviewing skill.

Suggestions include formalised approaches to learning how to accurately self-evaluate interviewing skills by utilising standardised instruments in combination with regular supervision.

Introduction

The recording of investigative interviews has increased the visibility and scrutiny faced by interviewers. For example, Smets and Rispens pointed out that "Nowadays, more and more emphasis is being brought to bear on the quality of interviews. In addition to this, with audio-visual recording and legal assistance during questioning, the investigative interviewing process is becoming increasingly transparent" (2014, p. 163). However, they noted that "investigative interviewing ... is not every police officer's strong suit" (p. 148). In many types of work, a belief in one's ability is necessary, especially when the stakes can be high, such as in medical and legal practice. Policing is no exception and Walsh and Milne (2007) found that experienced investigators viewed themselves as skilled interviewers. Unfortunately, there may sometimes be a meaningful difference between self-belief and more objective assessments of ability/performance. Although Walsh and Bull (2011) found that over 90% of those involved in the interviewing of suspects indicated that the PEACE method was useful, and many possessed awareness of the many skills required in skilled interviewing, this was not mirrored in actual interviews (conducted around the same time) (Walsh & Bull, 2010). Furthermore, "none of the supervisors ... had an evaluation framework to structure their assessments" (Walsh & Bull, p. 649). Walsh, King, and Griffiths (2017) compared 30 professional interviewers' self-assessments of their skills in a mock video-recorded interview with a suspect. For 24 of the 30 skills assessed, the self-ratings were significantly higher than the experts'. Indeed, the majority of the expert evaluations "fell below the level of satisfactory performance" (p. 657).

Assessments of various skills displayed in actual interviews with suspects can be unduly influenced by the "outcome" of each interview. For example, Bull and Cherryman (1996) found that police interviewers' evaluations of audio-recorded, real-life interviews with suspects conducted by other interviewers were influenced by whether or not a confession occurred. If police interviews are going to be more open to public scrutiny around the world as recommended by international guidelines (e.g., Mendez Principles,[1] then it is imperative that

DOI: 10.4324/9781003145998-7

assessors are not biased by outcomes, but instead ensure they rate appropriate evidence-based behaviours across the interview. Research studies evaluating actual interviews using police raters have used stringent, well-defined coding systems and training sessions to ensure inter-rater reliability across coders is of an acceptable scientific standard (e.g., Clarke et al., 2011). Consistency across assessment strategies is key, especially if used as part of an organisational staff appraisal system. It could be that across different countries, where investigative mindsets differ, where training regimes are at different stages in the investigative interviewing development process, police evaluators and interviewers themselves will be more or less influenced by outcomes (work is currently underway e.g., Chin et al., in submission). Having a standardised approach to assessment will go some way in addressing this potential bias and allow for meaningful comparison across jurisdictions.

In an attempt to improve interviewer self-assessments, Griffiths and Walsh (2018) asked the same interviewers as in their 2017 study to assess their interviews using "an extensive reflective log" and found that those whose own interviews had received an expert rating "as skilled" were more accurate using the log than those whose interviews had received lower expert ratings. Further, Smets and Rispens (2014) noted that

> some investigative interviewers are not able to differentiate their own interviewing behaviour from undesirable interviewing skills because they have no insight into their personal professional performance. Insight into professional performance is essential, both on the part of the trainer and the interviewer, before interview behaviour can be optimised.
>
> (p. 163)

Insight into one's own ability within the investigative interviewing arena has also emerged as a topic when examining the role that rapport and empathy play within successful interviews, especially with those deemed vulnerable (Risan et al., 2016). Research has now established that rapport is an important determinant of the quality of investigative interviews and is related to gaining accurate and reliable information from interviewees (e.g., Nunan et al., 2020). Key to being able to establish and maintain rapport across an interaction is the "management of one's own interpersonal responses and a fluid and organic response to another person" (Alison et al., 2021, p. 30), and this is based on "trust, empathy and a shared understanding of one another" (Alison et al., 2021, p. 34). To do this the interviewer needs to be "open-minded and curious rather than judgmental" (Alison et al., 2021, p. 34). There are a number of definitions of rapport (Bull & Baker, 2020), however there are common elements across them: mutual trust, respect, being genuine, and having a positive mindset. Rapport development and maintenance (Walsh & Bull, 2012a) thus requires being self-aware and able to manage one's own emotions, both concepts central to one's emotional intelligence (Risan et al., 2016). The appraisal of emotional expression and being able to respond appropriately is related to empathic understanding in a relationship, another facet under-pinning emotional intelligence (Risan et al., 2016). Relating this discussion back to supervision, in an in-depth evaluation of high stakes interviews with suspects and witnesses, Griffiths and Milne (2005) found that one of the key areas that distinguished advanced interviewers (e.g., Tier 3 interviewers in the UK—see Griffiths and Milne, 2005 and Chapter 4 of this book for further explanation) from the norm (Tier 2), was their ability to embody the more complex skills like rapport. It could be that only those able to reach the more advanced interviewing competence levels are also those more able to successfully assess interviewing standards as they have more insight and awareness. Indeed, one of facets of the Tier 5 role in the UK (i.e., "Interview Advisor"), is interview supervision; to quality assure Tier 3 interviewers (see Vaughan et al., in submission for explanation of the Tier 5 role).

It must be borne in mind that to become a Tier 5, applicants need to have undertaken and passed Tier 3 training (i.e., be an advanced interviewer).

Very little is publicly available on how supervisors can/should provide detailed and clear feedback regarding the interviewing of suspects per se, let alone vulnerable suspects. Of course, without valid and reliable ways of describing and assessing all of the relevant skills, effective feedback cannot take place. As outlined above, researchers have developed methods of assessing the skills involved in the interviewing of suspects for research purposes (e.g., rating scales: Clarke et al., 2011; GQM: Griffiths & Milne, 2005; quantifying observed tactics: Kelly et al., 2016; ORBIT: Alison et al., 2021).

However, in research, the majority of assessors are academics or practitioners studying for university qualifications under the supervision of an academic. If supervision is key and at the heart of achieving sustainable good practice (i.e., "E" of PEACE) then there needs to be a tool/instrument that ensures consistent assessment of interviews that practitioners can themselves utilise. One example could be the use of the behaviourally anchored rating scale (BARS) known in the occupational psychology literature for being less variable across raters and being more robust across situations (Smith & Kendall, 1963). In their national evaluation of the PEACE method of investigative interview training, Clarke and Milne (2001) developed the BARS-PEACE. To construct the BARS-PEACE, first a group of skilled police interviewers were asked to identify the interviewing "dimensions" to be assessed and then specify good and poor behaviours for each "dimension". Then another group of skilled police interviewers were provided with the 300 behaviours that the first group had identified and they had to allocate these to the "dimensions" and then rate the behaviours on a scale from 1–7 according to the appropriateness of the behaviour. A total of 11 "dimensions" consensually emerged involving a great variety of example behaviours, each of which could be put on a "behaviourally anchored rating scale". Next, using this assessment instrument, supervisors from several police organisations evaluated a sample of tape-recorded, real-life interviews to examine to what extent they could successfully use the new instrument. It was found that assessment consistency was not convergent across police raters even when given exemplar behaviours—the variation was largely a function of their own beliefs about what constitutes a "good" interview with a suspect (an overview of part of the evaluation is available in Clarke, Milne, and Bull, 2011). We have also developed methods of assessing the dozens of skills involved in the interviewing of suspects in some of our other work such as major analyses of interviews: (i) with 56 suspects of serious crimes (see https://leicester.figshare.com/articles/thesis/Police_Interviewing_of_Serious_Crime_Suspects/10125785); and (ii) with a large number of fraud suspects (Walsh & Bull, 2010, 2012a and b, 2015).

One aid to the supervision of interviews is to be aware of what typically occurs when interviewing vulnerable suspects. One of the few relevant more recent studies on assessing the interviewing of juvenile suspects is by Cleary and Warner (2016) who in the United States were able to get a large sample of experienced police investigators to complete a survey about the methods and skills they used when interviewing juvenile suspects. The skill rated highest was "building rapport" and among the lowest was "discouraging denials". In the middle of the ratings were "moving physically closer to suspect", "minimising seriousness of offence", and "using deceit". (A similar pattern of ratings was found for their interviewing of adult suspects, indicating little difference in self-reported usage for adult and juvenile suspects.) Of the 340 participants, 56% indicated that their training had involved the "Reid Technique" and Cleary and Warner (p. 278) found that "Reid trained officers were more likely to use manipulation techniques". Thus, for supervisors/senior managers a decision has to be made as to whether juvenile suspects are more vulnerable than adult suspects, and if they indeed are, what differences this should make to training and supervision. Another rare study on actual interviews with young suspects (average age of 12 years old) was conducted in Israel by Hershkowitz, Horowitz, Lamb, Orbach, and Sternberg (2004), who found that "interviewers used more risky (potentially error-inducing) prompts when interviewing suspects rather than alleged victims" (p. 423). Similarly, Winerdal, Cederborg, and Lindholm (2019) stated in their study of police interviews with juveniles (i.e., under the age of 18 years old) in Sweden that "the police officers' question style to a large extent contradicts recommendations" (p. 136). There is limited work examining real-life interviews with vulnerable suspects. Farrugia and Gabbert (2019) examined the practices of interviewers within 30 interviews with mentally disordered suspects and concluded that best practice guidance is not being fully adhered to. Officers were amending their behaviour to account for the vulnerability but were also using minimisation tactics, which is a concern due to heightened suggestibility within this population. Thus, regardless of type of interviewee, transference of research into practice is not yet fully realised.

Powell and Barnett (2015) emphasised that to maximise progress organisations need to consider the development of a coordinated quality improvement approach that involves not only practitioner feedback/supervision but also organisational evaluation. Mount and Mazerolle's (2020) study explored factors that influence the transfer of interviewing skills from the training environment to the real world. They found that (i) trainee motivation, (ii) perceptions of training relevance, (iii) perceptions of training quality, and (iv) preparedness to conduct the task as trained influence the degree to which such skills transfer to the police workplace. They noted that awareness of these factors is likely to help trainers and workplace managers to improve transfer rates and obtain more outcome value for the money, time, and effort invested in training.

In 2016, one of the leaders on improving the interviewing of vulnerable people noted that for over 30 years researchers and professionals have improved our relevant knowledge regarding how to interview and have, in light of this, developed training programmes (Lamb, 2016). However, he pointed out that studies have discovered that "widespread training has had a limited impact on the actual quality of interviews conducted in the field" (p. 710). He stressed that for knowledge transfer from research to practice to improve

> There is now clear evidence that improvements in interviewing practice occur reliably only when training courses involve multiple modules, distributed over time, with repeated opportunities for interviewers to consolidate learning and to obtain feedback on the quality of the interviews they do conduct
>
> (p. 710).

When discussing their findings regarding the interviewing of vulnerable suspects Geijsen, de Ruiter, and Kop (2018) stated that "Continued coaching and supervision of interrogations is essential, because police officers find it difficult to maintain complex social and communication skills" (p. 12). To this we could add that interviewers are much more likely to employ techniques and skills if they have been convinced of their practical effectiveness by people whom they trust and respect and are thus credible (Smets & Rispens, 2014).

To try and understand the discord between research and practice, Milne and Griffiths (2018) developed the Framework of Investigate Transformation (FIT) outlining eight factors or "enablers" they believe are necessary to develop competent investigative interviewers and unbiased investigative decision-makers. The first FIT factor is at the macro level: governments, international and national organisations, and legislators need to set the agenda by outlining the minimum standards of practice based on human rights principles. Examples of this are the Mendez Principles, and the *Police and Criminal Evidence Act* (1984: UK). The next four FIT factors are at the meso level and include the organisational factors of leadership, training regime, oversight, and use of technology. Leaders have to instil the right climate for change, learning from mistakes and embracing new legislation and guidance (e.g., miscarriages are often seen as a drive for change. See Poyser & Milne, 2021).

Any training programme needs to utilise pedagogical theory that maximises transference to real-life practice (see Chapter 4). Training in investigative interviewing needs to encapsulate scenario-based training, with small classes, with a high ratio of practice with expert feedback, including sessions that are immersive and reflect the real world that the investigators are about to encompass (Westera et al., 2019). Included in this is the slow acquisition of skills, across an interviewer's career, being taught more advanced methods as and when they require them for the more complex interviews, especially of those who are vulnerable (the Tiered system: Clarke and Milne, 2001; see Akca, Larivere, & Eastwood, 2021 for a systematic review). Training methods need to successfully embed over time the required skills and resist skills fade.

This leads onto the final two factors at the meso level: oversight and technology. Oversight includes supervision—the topic of this chapter. Without a formalised supervision policy in place, initiatives to substantially improve investigative interviewing across an organisation are likely to fail. This is where most well-meaning ventures fall short: due to time and money. Technology goes hand in hand with oversight. In order for adequate evaluation to take place the interview process needs to be transparent. A good example of this is the implementation of mandatory recording for every suspect interview in England and Wales (since 1986). This requirement has had a fundamental role in bringing about change (Bull, 2019; Bull & Rachlew, 2019). Other areas of policing are now seeing similarly increased levels of transparency through the use of body-worn cameras.

The final FIT factors are at the micro-level but are integral to the policy set at the meso level. Individual interviewers need to have the right skill set and ability in the first place, and adopt the appropriate mindset, especially at the more advanced levels. As mentioned above, not everyone will have the right levels of self-awareness and emotional intelligence to be able to successfully conduct the more difficult interviews. Investigative interviewing is a highly complex skill, and research has shown that not everyone has the ability, even with appropriate training regimes, to achieve this (Griffiths & Milne, 2018; see Acka & Eastwood, 2021 for exploratory work in the laboratory examining personality and investigative interviewing ability). Such micro-level factors are inextricably linked to interviewers' knowledge base garnered through research-informed training.

With regard to the questioning of vulnerable people, Hunter, Jacobson, and Kirby (2018) found judges in England and Wales recognised that although recently some professionals' skills were improving, there may well be a need for an appraisal system (for more on vulnerable people's participation in courts see Jacobson and Cooper, 2020). White, Bornman, Johnson, and Msipa (2020) noted that vulnerable people "continue to face significant barriers" (p. 2) regarding justice systems. In their substantial overview of over 50 prior publications they found four relevant factors, these being: (i) "respect" (i.e., treating vulnerable persons with dignity which includes adapting to their needs); (ii) "voice" (i.e., assisting vulnerable persons to communicate); (iii) "understanding" (i.e., ensuring vulnerable people understand what is happening); and (iv) "neutrality" (i.e., professionals not being biased)—supervisors and organisations need to be very aware of these factors.

Conclusion

In sum, there seems to be a mismatch between belief in their ability by practitioners and the reality of what is actually occurring in the field. Thus, there needs to be a joined-up way of thinking regarding what constitutes a "good" standard of interview that works in the field, by legislature, academics, and practitioners. At the heart of change are oversight mechanisms including supervision that need to be fair, transparent, and conducted by well-trained individuals who are specialists, using tools that ensure a consistent approach across assessed individuals, jurisdictions, and situations. This approach will lead to improved practices generally which is likely to have an even greater impact when it comes to interviewing vulnerable suspects.

Note

1 Available at https://www.wcl.american.edu/impact/initiatives-

References

Acka, D., & Eastwood, J. (2021). The impact of individual differences on investigative interviewing performance: A test of the police interviewing competencies inventory and the five factor model. *Police Practice and Research: An International Journal, 22*, 1027–1045.

Acka, D., Lanviere, C.D., & Eastwood, J. (2021). Assessing the efficacy of investigative interviewing training courses: A systematic review. *International Journal of Police Science and Management, 23*, 73-84. https://doi.org/10.1177%2F14613557211008470

Alison, L.J, Alison, E.K., Shortland, N.D., & Surman-Bohr, F. (2021). *ORBIT: The science of rapport-based interviewing for law enforcement, security and military*. Oxford University Press.

Bull, R. (2019). Roar or PEACE: Is it a tall story? In R. Bull & I. Blandon-Gitlin (Eds.), *International handbook of legal and investigative psychology*. Routledge.

Bull, R., & Baker, B. (2020). Obtaining from suspects valid discourse 'PEACE'-fully: What role for rapport and empathy? In M. Mason & F. Rock (Eds.), *The discourse of police interviews*. University of Chicago Press.

Bull, R., & Rachlew, A. (2019). Investigative interviewing: From England to Norway and beyond. In S. Barela, M. Fallon, G. Gaggioli, & J. Ohlin (Eds.), *Interrogation and torture: Research on efficacy, and its integration with morality and legality*. Oxford University Press.

Bull, R., & Cherryman, J. (1996). *Helping to identify skills gaps in specialist investigative interviewing: Enhancement of professional skills*. Home Office, Research, Development and Statistics Directorate.

Burrows, K.S., & Powell, M.B. (2014). Prosecutors' perceptions on improving child witness interviews about abuse. In R. Bull (Ed.), *Investigative interviewing* (pp. 229–242). Springer.

Clarke, C. & Milne, R. (2001). *National evaluation of the PEACE investigative interviewing course (PRAS; No. 149)*. Home Office. (PRAS; No. 149). Available at https://www.researchgate.net/publication/263127370_National_Evaluation_of_the_PEACE_Investigative_Interviewing_Course

Clarke, C., Milne, R., & Bull, R. (2011). Interviewing suspects of crime: The impact of PEACE training, supervision and the presence of a legal advisor. *Journal of Investigative Psychology and Offender Profiling, 8*(2), 149–162. https://doi.org/10.1002/jip.144

Cleary, H., & Warner, T.C. (2016). Police training in interviewing and interrogation methods: A comparison of techniques used with adult and juvenile suspects. *Law and Human Behavior, 40*(3), 270–284. https://doi.org/10.1037/lhb0000175

Farrugia, L., & Gabbert, F. (2019). Vulnerable suspects in police interviews: Exploring current practice in England and Wales. *Investigative Psychology and Offender Profiling, 17*, 17–30. https://doi.org/10.1002/jip.1537

Geijsen, K., de Ruiter, C., and Kop, N. (2018). Identifying psychological vulnerabilities: Studies on police suspects' mental health issues and police officers' views. *Cogent Psychology, 5*(1), 1462133. https://doi.org/10.1080/23311908.2018.1462133

Griffiths, A., and Milne, R. (2005). Will it all end in tiers? Police interviews with suspects in Britain. In T. Williamson (Ed.), *Investigative interviewing: Rights, research, regulation.* (pp. 167–189). Willan Publishing.

Griffiths, A., and Milne, R. (Eds.) (2018). *The psychology of criminal investigation; From theory to practice.* Routledge.

Griffiths, A., & Walsh, D. (2018). Qualitative analysis of qualitative evaluation: An exploratory examination of investigative interviewers' reflections on their performance. *Psychology, Crime & Law, 24*(4), 433–450. https://doi.org/10.1080/1068316X.2017.1390115

Hershkowitz, I., Horowitz, D., Lamb, M.E., Orbach, Y., & Sternberg, K.J. (2004). Interviewing youthful suspects in alleged sex crimes: A descriptive analysis. *Child Abuse & Neglect, 28*(4), 423–438. https://psycnet.apa.org/doi/10.1016/j.chiabu.2003.09.021

Hunter, G., Jacobson, J., & Kirby, A. (2018). *Judicial perceptions of the quality of criminal advocacy.* Report of Research Commissioned by the Solicitors Regulation Authority and the Bar Standards Board.

Jacobson, J., & Cooper, P. (Eds.) (2020). *Participation in courts and tribunals: concepts, realities and aspirations.* Bristol University Press.

Kelly, C.E., Miller, J.C., & Redlich, A.D. (2016). The dynamic nature of interrogation. *Law and Human Behavior, 40*(3), 296–309.

Lamb, M.E. (2016). Difficulties translating research on forensic interview practices to practitioners: Finding water, leading horses, but can we get them to drink? *American Psychologist, 71*(8), 710–718. https://doi.org/10.1037/amp0000039

Mount, D., & Mazerolle, L. (2020). Investigative interviewing skills in policing: examining the transfer of training into workplace practices. *Policing: An International Journal.* (Available online) http://doi.org/10.1108/pijpsm-12-2019-0182

Nunan, J., Stanier, I., Milne, R., Shawyer, A., Walsh, D., May. B. (2020). The impact of rapport on intelligence yield: Police source handler telephone interactions with covert human intelligence sources. *Psychiatry, Psychology and Law, 29*(1), 1–19.

Powell, M.B., & Barnett, M. (2015). Elements underpinning successful implementation of a national best-practice child investigative interviewing framework. *Psychiatry, Psychology and Law, 22*(3), 368–377. https://psycnet.apa.org/doi/10.1080/13218719.2014.951112

Poyser, S., and Milne, R. (2021). The time in between a case of 'wrongful' and 'rightful' conviction in the UK: Miscarriages of justice and the contributions of psychology to reform the police investigative process. *International Journal of Police Science and Management.* https://doi.org/10.1177%2F14613557211006134

Risan, P., Binder, P.E., and Milne, R. (2016). Emotional intelligence in police interviews- approach, training and usefulness of the concept. *Journal of Forensic Psychology Practice, 16*, 410–424. https://doi.org/10.1080/15228932.2016.1234143

Smith, P.C., & Kendall, L.M. (1963). Retranslation of expectations: An approach to the construction of unambiguous anchors for rating scales. *Journal of Applied Psychology, 47*(2), 149–155. https://doi.org/10.1037/h0047060

Smets, L., & Rispens, I. (2014). Investigative interviewing and training: The investigative interviewer apprentice. In R. Bull (Ed.), *Investigative interviewing* (pp. 147–165). Springer.

Walsh, D., & Bull, R. (2011). Benefit fraud investigative interviewing: Investigation professionals' beliefs concerning practice. *Journal of Investigative Psychology and Offender Profiling, 8*, 189–202. https://doi.org/10.1002/jip.137

Walsh, D., & Bull, R. (2015). The association between interview skills, questioning and evidence disclosure strategies, and interview outcomes. *Psychology, Crime and Law, 21*, 661–680. https://doi.org/10.1080/1068316X.2015.1028544

Walsh, D., & Bull, R. (2012a). Examining rapport in investigative interviews with suspects: Does its building and maintenance work? *Journal of Police and Criminal Psychology, 27*, 73–84. https://psycnet.apa.org/doi/10.1007/s11896-011-9087-x

Walsh, D., & Bull, R. (2012b). How do interviewers attempt to overcome suspects' denials? *Psychiatry, Psychology and Law, 19*, 151–168. https://psycnet.apa.org/doi/10.1080/13218719.2010.543756

Walsh, D., & Bull, R. (2010). Interviewing suspects of fraud: An in-depth analysis of interviewing skills. *Journal of Psychiatry and Law, 38*, 99–135. https://doi.org/10.1177%2F009318531003800106

Walsh, D., King, M., & Griffiths, A. (2017). Evaluating interviews which search for the truth with suspects: but are investigators' self-assessments of their own skills truthful ones? *Psychology, Crime & Law*, *23*(7), 647–665. https://doi.org/10.1080/1068316X.2017.1296149

Walsh, D., & Milne, R. (2007). Perceptions of benefit fraud staff in the UK: Giving PEACE a chance? *Public Administration*, *85*(2), 525–540. https://doi.org/10.1111/j.1467-9299.2007.00645.x

Westera, N., Powell, M., Milne, R., Goodman-Delahunty, J. (2019). Police organizational responses to interviewing victims of sexual offences. In R. Bull & I. Blandon-Gitlin (Eds.), *Handbook of legal and investigative psychology*. Routledge.

White, R., Bornman, J., Johnson, E., & Msipa, D. (2020). Court accommodations for persons with severe communication disabilities: A legal scoping review. *Psychology, Public Policy, and Law*, advanced copy online, https://psycnet.apa.org/doi/10.1037/law0000289

Winerdal, U., Cederborg, A.C., & Lindholm, J. (2019). The quality of question types in Swedish police interviews with young suspects of serious crimes. *The Police Journal*, *92*(2), 136–149. https://doi.org/10.1177%2F0032258X18770915

Part II

Chapter 6

Interviewing intoxicated suspects

Celine van Golde, Jane Tudor-Owen and David Gee

Executive summary

Intoxication through the use of alcohol or other drugs (AOD) is one of the most prominent issues within everyday policing. A vast number of arrests made on a daily basis involves intoxicated suspects. Intoxication leads to impairment of many functions such as inhibition, memory, and ability to resist suggestions. As such, intoxication increases the vulnerability of a suspect. However, it is difficult to assess a suspect's intoxication based on visual cues. There are individual differences between people's responses to alcohol and drugs. Moreover, it is difficult to determine what is causing the intoxication: alcohol, an illicit drug, a prescribed drug, or a combination of those.

Given that intoxication impacts various functions which are needed to ensure fairness in an interview, it is pertinent to determine the extent to which an intoxicated suspect's ability to participate in an interview is impaired. A series of questions can be asked which will help establish intoxication status. In turn a decision can be made to wait, or proceed, with an interview. In some cases, medical assistance needs to be provided. If the decision is made to proceed with the interview with an intoxicated person, extreme care needs to be taken to ensure fairness for the intoxicated suspect and the admissibility of any interview conducted.

This chapter will provide an overview of the relationship between intoxication and crime, perceptions of intoxicated suspects, vulnerabilities of intoxicated suspects, and implications for interviewing intoxicated suspects.

Introduction

Arguably one of the most common vulnerabilities that police officers will encounter during their daily activities is suspects who are under the influence of alcohol and/or other drugs (AOD) (Kloft et al., 2021; Monds et al., 2019). Indeed, when looking at data across the world we not only see a substantial consumption of AOD in the general population, we also more importantly see a strong link between intoxication and the occurrence of crime. Some countries even record that 50% of their reported assaults involve alcohol consumption (see Jores et al., 2019 for a review).

The effects that AOD intoxication has on people's behaviours and mental capacities create challenges for police officers. Most people are aware that intoxication will have an impact on—and most likely impair—someone's behaviour and their mental abilities. Decision making (good or bad), suggestibility, and executive functioning are just a few of the capacities that are impacted when someone is under the influence of an intoxicating substance (Kloft et al., 2021). In an informal setting, these effects of AOD are often the desired results and will not necessarily negatively impact the user. However, when it comes to forensic interviewing

DOI: 10.4324/9781003145998-9

settings, intoxication places a suspect in a vulnerable position and as such adjustments need to be made.

In this chapter, the relationship between crime and AOD will be discussed followed by the interactions with, and perceptions of, intoxicated suspects. These sections will be followed by an outline of vulnerabilities of intoxicated suspects, and considerations that should be taken when interviewing them. Lastly, recommendations regarding interview practices and a case study will be provided.

AOD and crime in numbers

Research has shown that alcohol consumption increases the risk of violence as much as 13.2 times within 24 hours of consumption (Haggård-Grann et al., 2006; Mindthoff et al., 2019. This increase in risk of violence by alcohol is reflected in crime statistics worldwide. In the United Kingdom (UK), almost half of violent crimes are committed by intoxicated persons. Similarly, in Sweden, between 50% and 70% of all violent crimes involve alcohol (Mindthoff et al., 2019). When McClelland and Teplin (2001) observed 2365 police encounters with citizens in the United States (US) they found that 34% of these encounters involved alcohol. Perpetrators in these observations were more likely to be intoxicated than victims. Similarly, an archival analysis of criminal case processes conducted by Palmer and colleagues (2013) in the United States showed that 29% of suspects were under the influence when committing a crime; most of them had been drinking alcohol.

However, not all drugs are the same. While the combination of alcohol with benzodiazepines results in a similar increased risk of violence as alcohol alone, benzodiazepines and antidepressants taken by themselves actually lower the risk of violent conduct (Haggård-Grann et al., 2006). While these drugs might have a positive effect regarding the reduction of violent conduct, their effects on a suspect's vulnerability can still be detrimental. This introduces another complexity when realising that different drugs can cause different vulnerabilities in suspects during interviews.

Interactions with, and perceptions of, intoxicated suspects

The relationship between AOD and crime is reflected in the experiences by police officers around the world. For example, when surveyed, Swedish officers said that intoxicated suspects were most likely to commit violent crimes, such as physical assault and general acts of violence (Hagsand et al., 2022). Moreover, when asked how often they interacted with intoxicated suspects, officers indicated that it was "common" (45%) or "very common" (42%) to interview intoxicated suspects (Hagsand et al., 2022). Similar numbers are reported by US police officers (Evans, 2009). When McNamare et al. (2017) looked at 327 criminal appellate court decisions in Australia in which evidence of intoxication was led, there were various points throughout the judicial process that intoxication of suspects was raised (e.g., whether intoxication was a contributing factor in offending; it negatively impacted mens rea, etc.). Importantly, they found that in 14 of the criminal cases the suspects were intoxicated during their interviews with police. The most reported substance in these cases was alcohol, however there was also some cannabis use, and some poly-substance use.

Vulnerabilities of intoxicated suspects

Intoxication by AOD might make suspects more vulnerable during interviews (Evans et al., 2009). However, how vulnerable intoxicated suspects really are and in what way is still being debated. Compared to *suspects*, we actually know more about the impact of intoxication on *witness* memory. For example, we know that low to midrange intoxication does not necessarily have a negative effect on witness memory, and that it is better to interview these intoxicated witnesses as soon as possible after witnessing the event, rather than waiting till they are sober (Hagsand et al., 2022; Jores et al., 2019; van Oorsouw & Broers, 2019). However, we cannot simply translate the research outcomes from intoxicated witnesses to intoxicated suspects.

Witnesses and suspects have different goals during an interview and therefore different vulnerabilities. While witnesses are mostly motivated to remember as much as possible to help the police, suspects might be more concerned about impression management (how they are perceived by police officers). Moreover, they might actually have the opposite motivation to hide or lie about what happened, or about their involvement (Hagsand et al., 2022). Because witnesses have a different role within crimes than suspects, they will focus or pay attention to different details. Their (direct) involvement also differs; consequently they will remember different things. Given that alcohol impacts all stages of memory (i.e., encoding, storage, and retrieval), but especially encoding, there is a high likelihood that intoxicated suspects might not remember what they did and therefore be especially susceptible to suggestion (Hagsand et al., 2022).

This is exactly what van Oorsouw et al. (2015) found when interviewing suspects who committed a mock crime while intoxicated three to five days after they committed this crime. They found that those who had been severely intoxicated when committing the crime were more suggestible compared to their sober counterparts. Similarly, van Oorsouw and Merckelbach (2012) using the same paradigm found that the more intoxicated the suspects were, the less details they could recall and the more errors they made. But it is not just errors and suggestions. Read and colleagues (1992) found that those that were intoxicated when committing a mock theft could recall less details of what they did, and who they saw, than those who were sober when committing the crime. However, if emotional arousal was very high while stealing, this actually minimised the impacts of alcohol intoxication on encoding and retrieval. In general, these mock suspects remembered less about what they exactly did, but were good at remembering what they saw.

One commonly used interviewing technique to detect lies is attempting to increase cognitive load in suspects (Vrij et al., 2008). That is, when cognitive load is increased in suspects, there is less cognitive capacity to produce and/or maintain lies. However, this technique can be especially problematic when interviewing intoxicated suspects. Rather than increasing truthfulness it might increase suggestibility, and consequently reduce the reliability of the information an intoxicated suspect provides. Besides potentially being more susceptible to suggestions, alcohol intoxication reduces inhibition and ability to consider future consequences. As such, intoxication might lead suspects to overshare sensitive information, including self-incriminating evidence (Hangsand et al., 2021). Evans (2009) interviewed US police officers who reported that intoxicated suspects were slightly more likely to waive their Miranda rights and incriminate themselves than sober suspects.

When memory loss (due to intoxication) happens, it can cause confusion and as such impact the ability of the suspect to deal with the interview. Additionally, intoxication makes it difficult to think clearly (Norfolk, 2001). However, even when this happens, it does not necessarily have to directly impact the self-perceived vulnerability of the suspect. During retrospective interviews with prisoners, it was very common for respondents to report that they were intoxicated both when they were committing the crimes, as well as during the police interviews. They further indicated that while intoxication made them confused during an interview, they self-reported that they were able to cope with the demand characteristics in the interview and intoxication was not one of the influencing reasons for a confession if they made one (Sigurdson & Gudjonson, 1994). Having these perceptions can actually increase vulnerability in suspects, as they will be less likely to ask for a break, a rest, or legal assistance.

This increase in vulnerability is reflected in research. In contrast with these self-reports, Pearse et al. (1998) found that suspects were three times as likely to confess during an interview by police if they reported using illicit drugs in the last 24 hours before the arrest, compared to those who did not use drugs. These confessions were not necessarily false, but the risk is that when suspects are intoxicated, they might misinterpret evidence against them, and are more inclined to confess. When it comes to suggestibility and illicit drug use, and the evidence directly linking various drugs to suggestibility and false memory formation, less is known. Kloft and colleagues (2022) found that when suspects were under the influence of MDMA when committing a (mock) crime, they were found to have increased vulnerability to suggestive questions only (Kloft et al., 2022). Being under the influence of cannabis when committing a mock crime was found to increase susceptibility to false memories (Kloft et al., 2019; 2020).

Lastly, it is not just intoxication which can cause vulnerability; withdrawal symptoms can create problems for suspects in interviews as well. Specifically, alcohol withdrawal might happen when in custody because there is no access to the substance (Norfolk, 2001). Gudjonson and colleagues in 2002 found that inpatients going through alcohol withdrawal were more suggestible, more cognitively impaired, and more anxious than those who were not going through withdrawal. They concluded that those going through withdrawal might be at a possible disadvantage when being interviewed. Withdrawal symptoms usually start within 12–48 hours after consumption of the last drink, but can start as early as 6 hours after, depending on the addiction. Alcohol withdrawal is associated with "anxiety, depression, irritability and transient hallucinations", all which can affect the interview of the suspect. A more serious side effect of withdrawal is delirium. This usually starts 72–96 hours after consumption of the last drink. "Delirium causes impaired attention and memory, disorganised thinking. Disorientation, reduced levels of consciousness, perceptual disturbances and agitation" (Norfolk, 2001, p. 9). As such, a suspect experiencing delirium should definitely not be interviewed and instead requires medical attention.

The effects of withdrawal vary depending on the drug itself. Sigurdson and Gudjonson (1994) found that most confessions are actually reliable depending on the type of drug withdrawal. There is, however, some evidence that those withdrawing from opiates are more suggestible and thus might make more unreliable confessions (Davidson & Gossop, 1996). However, the confessions may also not be reliable due to suspects believing that a confession will expedite their release and they will therefore be able to use drugs more quickly. As such, their withdrawal is an indirect motivator to falsely confess (Davidson & Gossop, 1996). In sum, when suffering from mild withdrawal symptoms, suspects can be interviewed. However, when suffering from severe withdrawal symptoms, the interview should be postponed till withdrawal subsides (Norfolk,2001).

Implications for interviews

Despite concerns regarding interviewing intoxicated suspects, it remains common practice. Police surveys indicated that while it was reportedly common to very common to encounter intoxicated suspects (Evans, 2009; Hagsand et al., 2022), police departments around the world, but also within the same country, differ in procedures on when, and how, to conduct interviews with suspects that are intoxicated. The inconsistency of these guidelines begins with limited consensus on how to assess if a suspect is intoxicated. Breathalyser tests are not typically conducted for the purpose of a standard interview (Hagsand et al., 2022; Monds et al., 2019); rather, there is a reliance on using visual cues (Evans et al., 2009; Monds et al., 2019).

Specifically, the majority of police officers surveyed did not use breathalysers for every suspect they believed was intoxicated (Evans, 2009; Hagsand et al., 2022). Other measures used included: "starting a conversation to assess intoxicating levels"; "ask suspects to self-report how many drinks they have had"; "use standard field sobriety tests (such as asking to walk in a straight line)"; and "behavioural cues (does the suspect, look or smell drunk)" (Hagsand et al., 2022, p. 10). However, there are issues with these methods.

Hagsand and colleagues (2022) noted that asking how many drinks a suspect has consumed might not be indicative of intoxication levels, as any two people might have different physical responses to the same amount of alcohol. Moreover, while measures might be useful to determine if a recreational drinker is intoxicated and potentially how severe, this is not the case for those with AOD abuse problems. Specifically, those who are addicted to alcohol can show no "regular" signs of intoxication while having a very high Blood Alcohol Content. Moreover, various of these signs of "intoxication" could be indicative of other impairments (e.g., cognitive or physical disabilities). Therefore, extreme caution should be taken when relying on these measures to determine intoxication.

When it comes to the actual interview, Evans (2009) showed that 65% of surveyed US police officers said the interviewing procedures they used for intoxicated suspects were the same as for sober ones. Similarly, there are no standardised guidelines for interviewing suspects in either the UK, the US, or Sweden (Hagsand et al., 2022). Even though guidelines for interviewing intoxicated suspects might be missing worldwide, officers in various countries know and indicate that they adjust their interviewing techniques in these situations. In Sweden, 60% of officers said they adjusted their interviewing procedures (Hagsand, 2022), while 32% of officers in the United States indicated they did this too (Evans, 2009). The adjustments that officers made were actions such as letting intoxicated suspects sleep or sober up before starting an official interview. One of the reasons officers said they preferred suspects to be sober was that they thought it was important that suspects were aware of what was happening during the interview.

Interview guidelines

There is evidence to suggest that it is common to interview suspects who may be intoxicated. The level of their intoxication is what will ultimately determine the extent to which the interview may or may not be considered voluntary and fair, including any confessional material obtained during the course of that interview.

As discussed, it is important to not only consider what has been ingested, but how it affects the specific individual. To that end, there are a series of questions which, when asked during the preamble of the interview, will at least provide a record of the interviewer's intention to ensure a fair and voluntary interview:

- Ask the suspect if they have consumed alcohol that day. Probe as to when their last drink was and how much they have had in the previous 24 hours.
- Question how this compares to an ordinary day for them.
- Ask if that amount of alcohol would usually affect their ability to have a conversation with someone.
- Query if they feel able to have a conversation at this time.
- Repeat with regard to drugs (illicit and prescription).

Capturing these antecedents will ultimately inform the prosecution and the judiciary as to whether the interview, or parts contained therein, are admissible. When there is any concern that the suspect may not be fit to interview, stop. In many jurisdictions there is a period for which an arrested person can be held in custody without charge. Provide the suspect with a drink, meal, and the opportunity to have a sleep before re-assessing their fitness for interview, bearing in mind what has previously been noted with regard to the impact of withdrawal.

Case study

As distinct from many jurisdictions, the UK has introduced the role of Custody Officer, who has a legal responsibility to ensure that the detention of an individual is necessary and that while being detained their legal and medical rights are protected. This postholder cannot take part in any investigation and represents the rights of the detainee within the legal framework. In the UK there are guidelines highlighting the importance of considering intoxication as a factor in determining whether a suspect may be interviewed (see e.g., College of Policing Authorised Professional Practice, 2021; Home Office Interviewing Suspects, 2020).

Clearly an interview of a detainee under the influence of any substance would be prohibited unless a failure to do so risked a threat to life. Custody staff have to assess detainees on two fronts: fitness to be detained and fitness for interview. Very often this has to be a judgement call on a case-to-case basis. Custody officers cannot be expected to be fully competent in either assessment from a medically trained perspective. The emphasis under challenge is for the Custody Officer to show that in their opinion the detainee was fit for interview. In making that deliberation it will be necessary for them to demonstrate that they took all reasonable steps in considering the question. Other influencing factors include the detention clock (how long a person can be held in custody before a review is required). During this time the Custody Officer has to ensure that the investigation is being actively progressed.

Conclusion

Given the statistics concerning AOD intoxication and crime, there is a high likelihood that an intoxicated suspect will be encountered during daily duties. Intoxication can impact cognitive functions such as memory, inhibition, suggestibility, and more. All these factors will influence the suspect's access to justice. Intoxicated suspects might be more vulnerable to not making the best decisions regarding participation in an interview, self-incrimination, and they might be more suggestible. All these vulnerabilities should be taken into account when a decision is made on interviewing an intoxicated person.

Always ask the above suggested questions to determine if a suspect is intoxicated, even when there are no visible signs. Especially those who have AOD dependency can show no signs of intoxication while under the influence. Timing of the interview might be important, and as such a decision can be made to proceed with an interview with an intoxicated suspect. Research above has shown that this does not have to be problematic, depending on the level of intoxication. Regardless, extreme care should be taken when interviewing an intoxicated person in order to accommodate for AOD-induced vulnerabilities.

References

Davison, S., & Gossop, M. (1996). The problem of interviewing drug addicts in custody: A study of interrogative suggestibility and compliance. *Psychology, Crime and Law*, *2*(3), 185–195.

Evans, J.R., Schreiber Compo, N., & Russano, M.B. (2009). Intoxicated witnesses and suspects: Procedures and prevalence according to law enforcement. *Psychology, Public Policy, and Law*, *15*(3), 194.

Gudjonsson, G., Hannesdottir, K., Petursson, H., & Bjornsson, G. (2002). The effects of alcohol withdrawal on mental state, interrogative suggestibility and compliance: An experimental study. *The Journal of Forensic Psychiatry*, *13*(1), 53–67.

Haggård-Grann, U., Hallqvist, J., Långström, N., & Möller, J. (2006). The role of alcohol and drugs in triggering criminal violence: A case-crossover study. *Addiction*, *101*(1), 100–108.

Hagsand, A.V., Evans, J.R., Pettersson, D., & Schreiber Compo, N. (2022). A survey of police officers encounters with sober, alcohol-and drug-intoxicated suspects in Sweden. *Psychology, Crime & Law*, *28:5*, 1–22.

Irving, B., & Hilgendorf, L. (1980). *Police interrogation: A case study of current practice*. HM Stationery Office.

Jores, T., Colloff, M.F., Kloft, L., Smailes, H., & Flowe, H.D. (2019). A meta-analysis of the effects of acute alcohol intoxication on witness recall. *Applied Cognitive Psychology*, *33*(3), 334–343.

Kloft, L., Otgaar, H., Blokland, A., Garbaciak, A., Monds, L.A., & Ramaekers, J.G. (2019). False memory formation in cannabis users: A field study. *Psychopharmacology*, *236*(12), 3439–3450.

Kloft, L., Otgaar, H., Blokland, A., Monds, L.A., Toennes, S.W., Loftus, E.F., & Ramaekers, J.G. (2020). Cannabis increases susceptibility to false memory. *Proceedings of the National Academy of Sciences*, *117*(9), 4585–4589.

Kloft, L., Monds, L.A., Blokland, A., Ramaekers, J.G., & Otgaar, H. (2021). Hazy memories in the courtroom: A review of alcohol and other drug effects on false memory and suggestibility. *Neuroscience & Biobehavioral Reviews*, *124*, 291–307.

Kloft, L., Otgaar, H., Blokland, A., Toennes, S.W., & Ramaekers, J.G. (2022). Remembering Molly: Immediate and delayed false memory formation after acute MDMA exposure. *European Neuropsychopharmacology*, *57*, 59–68.

McClelland, G.M., & Teplin, L.A. (2001). Alcohol intoxication and violent crime: Implications for public health policy. *The American Journal on Addictions*, *10*, s70–s85.

McNamara, L.U.K.E., Quilter, J., Seear, K., & Room, R. (2017). Evidence of intoxication in Australian criminal courts: A complex variable with multiple effects. *Monash University Law Review*, *43*(1), 148–194.

Mindthoff, A., Hagsand, A.V., Schreiber Compo, N., & Evans, J.R. (2019). Does alcohol loosen the tongue? Intoxicated individuals' willingness to report transgressions or criminal behavior carried out by themselves or others. *Applied Cognitive Psychology*, *33*(3), 414–425.

Monds, L.A., Quilter, J., Van Golde, C., & McNamara, L. (2019). Police as experts in the detection of alcohol and other drug intoxication: A review of the scientific evidence within the Australian legal context. *University of Queensland Law Journal*, *38*(2), 367–388.

Norfolk, G. (2001). Fit to be interviewed by the police: An aid to assessment. *Medicine, Science and the Law*, *41*(1), 5–12.

van Oorsouw, K., & Merckelbach, H. (2012). The effects of alcohol on crime-related memories: A field study. *Applied Cognitive Psychology*, *26*(1), 82–90.

van Oorsouw, K., Merckelbach, H., & Smeets, T. (2015). Alcohol intoxication impairs memory and increases suggestibility for a mock crime: A field study. *Applied Cognitive Psychology*, *29*(4), 493–501.

van Oorsouw, K., Broers, N.J., & Sauerland, M. (2019). Alcohol intoxication impairs eyewitness memory and increases suggestibility: Two field studies. *Applied Cognitive Psychology*, *33*(3), 439–455.

Palmer, F.T., Flowe, H.D., Takarangi, M.K., & Humphries, J.E. (2013). Intoxicated witnesses and suspects: An archival analysis of their involvement in criminal case processing. *Law and Human Behavior*, *37*(1), 54.

Pearse, J., Gudjonsson, G.H., Clare, I.C.H., & Rutter, S. (1998). Police interviewing and psychological vulnerabilities: Predicting the likelihood of a confession. *Journal of Community & Applied Social Psychology*, *8*(1), 1–21.

Read, J.D., Yuille, J.C., & Tollestrup, P. (1992). Recollections of a robbery: Effects of arousal and alcohol upon recall and person identification. *Law and Human Behavior*, *16*(4), 425.

Sigurdsson, J.F., & Gudjonsson, G.H. (1994). Alcohol and drug intoxication during police interrogation and the reasons why suspects confess to the police. *Addiction*, *89*(8), 985–997.

Vrij, A., Fisher, R., Mann, S., & Leal, S. (2008). A cognitive load approach to lie detection. *Journal of Investigative Psychology and Offender Profiling*, *5*(1–2), 39–43.

Chapter 7

Interviewing older adult suspects

Celine van Golde, Jane Tudor-Owen and David Gee

Executive summary

The number of older adults worldwide is increasing and so is the number of older adult offenders. Ageing comes with an increase in a range of social and psychological vulnerabilities, which means older adult suspects should be considered especially vulnerable when being interviewed. However, unlike juvenile offenders, no standard accommodations are made for older adults. Diseases such as Alzheimer's and Dementia can make suspects forgetful and confused. Moreover, heightened emotions can impact the ability to participate in legal processes. This puts older adult suspects at risk when navigating the criminal justice system, impacting their access to justice.

As suspects approach older age (e.g., over 50), attention must be paid to the potential for cognitive decline, and brief screening questions should be asked to establish if they are capable of participating in an interview. When in doubt, a full mental health assessment by a professional should be conducted. If an interview takes place, small adjustments can be made to ensure fairness for the older adult suspect. This chapter will provide an overview of older adults in society, their vulnerabilities as suspects, perceptions of older adult offenders, and implications for interviewing older adult suspects.

Introduction

Determining who is categorised as an "older adult" might not be as straightforward as it seems. The United Nations classifies an older adult as anyone over 60 years of age, while researchers studying older adults and the process of ageing (i.e., gerontologists) consider those over 65 as older adults (Merkt et al., 2020). Given these two ages are not too far apart it seems an easy check when interviewing a person who appears to be an older adult. Take a quick look at the suspect's identification, and if they are over 60 take their age into consideration when interviewing them.

However, when focusing on research of older adult offenders specifically, the cut-off age to be classified as an older adult is drastically lower. That is, when Merkt and colleagues (2020) conducted a systematic review trying to determine an age cut-off, they found that when looking at older offenders and prisoners specifically, any suspect in the criminal justice system over 50 years of age should be considered an older adult. The research reviewed showed a decline in cognitive functioning, an increase in mental health issues, and shorter life expectancies in offenders and prisoners over 50 compared to community members. This is an important distinction as it is these characteristics that will increase vulnerability during interviews. As such, the advice given in this chapter should not just be applied to those who

DOI: 10.4324/9781003145998-10

would be considered senior citizens in the community; when a suspect is over 50 years of age there should be some awareness of the potential for cognitive decline, although it would not be the norm.

When we look at the population worldwide an interesting development appears: the world is getting older. The United Nations reported in 2019 that worldwide 703 million people were over the age of 65. This number represented 9% of the world population and was a 3% increase since 1990 (United Nations, 2019). The projected growth of the older adult population is exponential, with the World Health Organization (WHO) predicting that one in six people will be classified as older adults (aged over 60) by 2030, which will be the equivalent of 1.4 billion people. Notably, this number will in turn roughly double by 2050 (World Health Organization, 2021). Simply put, people are living longer. Notably, in the near future a negative population growth is predicted, where the number of births will be lower than the number of deaths (Kratcoski & Edelbacher, 2021). For example, Kratcoski and Edelbacher (2018) pointed out that this will result in more people over 65 years of age than people under 18 years of age living in the United States by 2030.

When looking at these developments as a whole, there are concerns that this disproportionate growth of the number of older adults compared to the declining numbers of younger people will create challenges for societies worldwide (UN, 2019), and especially for mid- and low-income countries (UN, 2019; WHO, 2021). These challenges include financial strains due to fewer people generating income. At the same time, financial resources will be drained as more people will be relying on these resources due to being at a retirement age. Maybe even more importantly, these challenges will also be felt regarding social resources. For example, older adults often report feeling more isolated once they retire (Kratcoski & Edelbacher, 2021), and there are increases in certain mental and physical health issues due to old age (e.g., depression, Alzheimer's, and physical disabilities; Tyuse et al., 2017). Further, with older people living longer, there are more opportunities to display behaviours which are undesirable (Kratcoski & Edelbacher, 2018). Specifically, when people in general live longer, offenders will too, and they will therefore have more time and opportunities to commit crimes.

This chapter begins with a profile of the older offender, and perceptions of older offenders in the criminal justice system. These sections will be followed by considerations when interviewing older suspects and recommendations for modification of standard interview practices.

The older offender

Just like younger offenders, older offenders are capable of committing any crime (Barak et al., 1995; Berger, 2019). They are arrested for committing white-collar or financial crimes (e.g., fraud, embezzlement), drug and alcohol-related crimes (e.g., DUI), as well as violent crimes (e.g., assault, murder). The types of crimes older offenders commit are heavily influenced by situational and personal factors, and interact with the person being a long term, or first term, offender (Berger, 2019; Kratcoski & Edelbacher, 2021). That is, those that have committed crimes all their life will keep on doing this if the opportunity, and ability to do so, is there. For example, there is a high likelihood that a child sex offender will keep on offending if the opportunity is there. Similarly, if an older white-collar criminal has the opportunity to commit insurance fraud they are likely to do this. Their previous experience, opportunity, and ability will enable them to keep on reoffending. At the same time, if opportunities and abilities change due to ageing, offenders often slow down and/or change the crimes they commit as they are no longer able to commit similar crimes anymore (Kratcoski, 2018).

On the other hand, first time older adult offenders are often driven by social and physical factors when committing crimes. For example, Bourget and colleagues (2010) found that in cases where older adult perpetrators committed homicides, mental health issues (such as depression, schizophrenia, Alzheimer's) more often than not played a role. At the same time, they stated that social pressures, such as no longer being able to care for their chronically ill partners, could contribute to these homicides as well. When ageing, the onset and increase of physical and mental ailments can result in offending behaviours (Berger, 2019; Barak et al., 1995). For example, a person with dementia may get confused and forget to pay when taking products from a shop, which constitutes shoplifting. While the behaviour is criminal, the intent behind these actions should be questioned given the mental state of the offender. More importantly, the crime would not have been committed if the person had not developed a psychiatric disorder due to old age (Bourns, 2000; Brown et al., 2014).

Regardless of being a first time, or long time, offender, ageing impacts the physical and social ability to commit certain crimes, and as such, the most reported crimes for older adults are fraud, drunk driving, and theft (Berger, 2019; Kratcoski, 2018; Kratcoski & Edelbacher, 2021). All these crimes have strong social and psychological determinants which are especially common amongst older adults (Kratcoski, 2018; Kratcoski & Edelbacher, 2021). High rates of depression are reported in older adult populations (Fazel et al., 2002; Tyuse et al., 2017). This will affect drinking and (prescription) drug use, which in turn can impact offending behaviours (e.g., DUI; Berger, 2019). Similarly, once retired, the loss of a steady income can result in older adults stealing or committing fraud (Kratcoski & Edelbacher, 2021). Diseases such as Alzheimer's and Dementia make people forgetful, or unaware of socially appropriate behaviour which can lead to stealing, or public disorder (Bourns, 2000; Brown et al., 2014). Importantly, both these social and psychological factors can cause emotional distress in general, but even more so when interacting with, and being interviewed by, the police. This is especially true for first-time offenders—given they have never come into contact with the police in this capacity before—and those who do not know where they are (i.e., people with Dementia; Bourns, 2000; Brown et al., 2014). As such, special care needs to be taken when interviewing older suspects.

Perceptions of older offenders

As mentioned above our world is getting older, and so are offenders. This results in an increase in offending rates amongst older adults, purely by the fact that there are more people over 65 alive than ever before (Berger, 2019). While there is a clear increase in offences committed by older adults, this is not as strongly reflected in the perceptions held by the general public and law enforcement personnel. Berger (2019), using a survey and semi-structured interviews, found that people believed in general that younger people were more likely to commit crimes than older people. However, when splitting these beliefs up between older (>60 years of age) and younger (<40 years of age) respondents, they found that especially those over 60 years of age believed older adults were less likely to commit crimes. Those under 40 believed older adults were actually more likely to commit white-collar crimes. When all were asked if they thought crimes amongst the older adults would increase in the coming years all participants agreed this would be the case.

When it comes to police officers' perceptions, there is a tendency to be more sympathetic towards older offenders (Kratcoski, 2018). With regard to crimes such as shoplifting, public intoxication, and domestic violence, police officers indicated that they believed these were more likely to be committed because of mental confusion than criminal intent (Fattah & Sacco, 1989). The perceptions that police officers hold might be related to the frequency they interact with older adults. When Brown and colleagues (2014) asked police officers in San Francisco, United States, about interactions with older adults, they found that 89% of the respondents said that they interacted at least monthly with older adults. Forty-one percent said they interacted with them on a weekly basis, and 19% on a daily basis. While these findings indicate that a large proportion of those police officers have regular interactions with older adults, they also indicated that they were not too certain about their abilities to interact with older adults, and specifically older offenders. Three-quarters of those interviewed were comfortable to determine if there were any barriers to communication with older adults (for example, if they had any hearing issues); however, most were not certain what the appropriate next steps were after identifying an issue. The biggest issues police officers saw were the need to make a distinction between whether a behaviour was criminal, or the result of a medical and/or psychological problem, and consequently how to deal with this.

Implications for interviews

In order to determine whether consideration needs to be paid to vulnerability associated with older adulthood, the suspect's age must be known. Consider that even those under 60 but over 50 should be assumed to be an older adult, and therefore may be more vulnerable. Especially when it comes to indigenous suspects (discussed in Chapter 11), those aged 50 and over should be treated as older given their overall life expectancy (Merkt et al., 2020). Once you have established that the suspect is older, you should identify if there are any clear impairments or illnesses you should take into consideration. A good guideline to follow when interacting with older people is to slow down in order to assess and respond to any of these impairments (Brown et al., 2014). These can be physical impairments (such as hearing or mobility impairments; see Chapter 13); cognitive impairments, or medical illness. Depending on the interviewer's observations, a decision may need to be made as to whether a suspect needs to receive medical attention before being interviewed.

Interview guidelines

While police officers are not trained medical or psychological specialists, there are some questions that may assist in determining the mental capacity of an older adult suspect. These questions should focus on current facts, as people with Dementia and Alzheimer's, for example, are better able to remember past- and well-rehearsed facts (such as their name, or date of birth), rather than current ones. This means they can come across as unimpaired, while they actually are. Instead, asking the day of the week or if the suspect knows what month it is will help determine in a very rudimentary way whether there may be a concern with regard to mental capacity. Specifically, if they are not able to answer these questions correctly, or they seem confused or avoid answering, it is important to seek a (mental) health assessment before conducting an interview.

Suspects with Alzheimer's Disease and older adult suspects in general may become emotional when being interviewed by the police. Older first offenders can be very ashamed, uncertain, and thus vulnerable during an interview (Barak et al., 1995). Older offenders often show a combination of behavioural, medical, and mental health conditions, putting them even more at risk (Metzger et al., 2017). It is therefore interesting to see that while most criminal acts worldwide make distinction on age when it concerns juveniles, this is not the case when it comes to older adults (Kratcoski, & Edelbacher, 2018). It is important to be aware that older adults might not understand their rights, or questions you ask them, but do not indicate this due to shame or fear (Barak et al., 1995). At the same time, due to inhibitory impairments they might make decisions and answer questions which are not in their best interest. Both these impairments might result in false confessions. Asking the older adult suspect to explain their rights back in their own words can provide a safeguard that they truly understand their rights. Additionally, building rapport is the most useful tool in not only assessing the extent and direction of an older adult suspect's vulnerabilities, but to further develop a plan in how to counteract these during the interview.

Dementia and Alzheimer's affect older adults proportionately more than younger. Both these disorders have a negative effect on memory, decision making, mood, and inhibition. In an interview setting, it might be difficult for older adults suspects with these disorders to act in their own best interest. The American Alzheimer's Association has suggested guidelines to follow when you encounter a person with Alzheimer's (Bourns, 2000):

- It is important to approach a person with Alzheimer's from the front.
- When speaking to them it is very important that you speak in a non-threatening way, using a low-pitched voice.
- Make sure to properly introduce yourself, and that the suspect registers this introduction.
- Avoid noisy settings and/or crowds when holding the conversation. When a person with Alzheimer's is in an unfamiliar situation or speaking to strangers, they are inclined to mimic body language and tone. Be aware that this can happen.
- Make sure that you are firm but not aggressive when interacting with an older adult who may have Alzheimer's.
- When it comes to interviewing, avoid an overload of instructions as this can easily confuse the suspect.
- Make sure to only ask one question at a time, and if needed use "yes" or "no" questions mostly.
- One common mistake made when interviewing a person with Alzheimer's, and older adult suspects in general, is to raise the voice (or shout). While this may help the hearing impaired it does not benefit other older suspects' understanding of what is asked from them (Bourns, 2000).

Conclusion

There is no single standard older adult suspect. Just like younger suspects they can commit any crime. Older adult suspects are, however, different when it comes to the reasons they commit crime. Especially in older adult first-time offenders a strong relationship with psychological impairments can be seen. As such, interviewing an older adult suspect can be challenging, given the range of social and psychological vulnerabilities that come with increased age. However, it is important to remember that many of these vulnerabilities can be accommodated when using proper investigative interviewing techniques. Use some of the strategies described above when speaking to an older adult suspect. Focus on building rapport; emotions can be heightened in older suspects, especially if they are first-time offenders. Ensuring that the older adult suspect feels comfortable will facilitate the interview.

References

Barak, Y., Perry, T., & Elizur, A. (1995). Elderly criminals: A study of the first criminal offence in old age. *International Journal of Geriatric Psychiatry, 10*(6), 511–516.

Berger, R. (2019). Criminal geropsychology: The nexus of elderly offending, mental disorders, and victimization. *Voice of the Publisher, 5*(3), 35.

Bourget, D., Gagné, P., & Whitehurst, L. (2010). Domestic homicide and homicide-suicide: The older offender. *Journal of the American Academy of Psychiatry and the Law Online, 38*(3), 305–311.

Bourns, W.F. (2000). Police gerontology services for the elderly: A policy guide. *Criminal Justice Studies, 13*(2), 179–192.

Brown, R.T., Ahalt, C., Steinman, M.A., Kruger, K., & Williams, B.A. (2014). Police on the front line of community geriatric health care: Challenges and opportunities. *Journal of the American Geriatrics Society, 62*(11), 2191–2198.

Fattah, E., & Sacco, V. (1989). *Crimes and victimization of the elderly*. Springer: New York.

Fazel, S., Hope, T., O'Donnel, I., & Jacoby, R. (2002). Psychiatric, demographic and personality characteristics of elderly sex offenders. *Psychological Medicine, 32*(2), 219–226.

World Health Organization (2021). Ageing and Health. https://www.who.int/news-room/fact-sheets/detail/ageing-and-health. Retrieved March 2022.

Kratcoski, P.C. (2018). Justice system response to elderly criminality. In *Perspectives on elderly crime and victimization* (pp. 197–224). Springer.

Kratcoski, P.C., & Edelbacher, M. (2021). Perspectives on elderly crime and victimization in the future. In *Crime prevention and justice in 2030* (pp. 85–106). Springer.

Merkt, H., Haesen, S., Meyer, L., Kressig, R.W., Elger, B.S., & Wangmo, T. (2020). Defining an age cut-off for older offenders: A systematic review of literature. *International Journal of Prisoner Health*.

Metzger, L., Ahalt, C., Kushel, M., Riker, A., & Williams, B. (2017). Mobilizing cross-sector community partnerships to address the needs of criminal justice-involved older adults: A framework for action. *International Journal of Prisoner Health*.

Tyuse, S.W., Cooper-Sadlo, S., & Underwood, S.E. (2017). Descriptive study of older adults encountered by crisis intervention team (CIT) law enforcement officers. *Journal of Women & Aging, 29*(4), 281–293.

United Nations, Department of Economic and Social Affairs, Population Division (2019). World Population Ageing 2019: Highlights (ST/ESA/SER.A/430).

World Population Ageing 2019: Highlights. https://www.un.org/en/development/desa/population/publications/pdf/ageing/WorldPopulationAgeing2019-Highlights.pdf. Retrieved, March, 2022.

Chapter 8

Children as suspects

Celine van Golde, Jane Tudor-Owen and David Gee

Executive summary

Juvenile suspects in the legal system should be considered especially vulnerable. There are many social and cognitive abilities that are still developing throughout the teen years, which place juveniles at high risk during interviews. Juveniles are more compliant (even when they get arrested) than adults, they are more suggestible, and as such have an increased risk of self-incrimination and false confessions. Moreover, due in part to their lack of experience, they have impaired legal understanding.

As such, juveniles should be protected during interviews. Adjustments should be made to interviewing methods used with adults (i.e., the PEACE model), to accommodate juveniles' vulnerabilities. Careful consideration should be given to the wording of questions asked during the interview. Additionally, support persons or Appropriate Adults should be provided to assist the juvenile during the interview. This person should at least be advising the juvenile and assisting the juvenile suspect with communication if needed. By introducing these safeguards, the juvenile suspect's needs can be protected during an interview, thereby improving their access to justice. This chapter will provide an overview of the vulnerabilities of juvenile suspects (i.e., suggestibility, waiving their rights, and self-incrimination), implications for interviewing juvenile suspects, a case study, and interview guidelines.

Introduction

There is a dearth in the availability of experimental research on interviewing juvenile offenders (17 years of age and younger; Redlich et al., 2004). This is surprising given that there are a vast number of youths who end up within the legal system each year. For example, in the United States almost 2.5 million juveniles were arrested in the year 2000. Almost one third of those arrested were not even 14 years old (Snyder, 2002 as cited by Redlich et al., 2004). However, all of those arrested would have been interviewed (either formally or informally) by police. Importantly, youth is a well-established vulnerability during interviews (e.g., Cleary, 2014; Feld, 2006).

The developmental vulnerabilities of juveniles are reflected in crime statistics. For example, juvenile exonerees were three times as likely to have falsely confessed to a crime than adult exonerees (Gross et al., 2005). Moreover, Malloy et al. (2014) found that one-third of a sample of 193 incarcerated juveniles reported to have either made a false confession or entered a false guilty plea. The main reason these detainees provided for their false confession or guilty plea was the use of coercive (high pressure) interview techniques and the long duration of their interviews (>2 hours). These findings are consistent with research that indicates juveniles' accounts (and false confessions) are more heavily affected by suggestive questions than

DOI: 10.4324/9781003145998-11

those of adults (e.g., Redlich & Goodman, 2003). It is therefore essential that interviewing techniques take into account a suspect's youth.

However, it is not just interviewing techniques that should be adjusted. Juveniles' understanding of their rights (and when to waive them) might be impaired due to developmental vulnerabilities as well (Abramovitch et al., 1993; Feld, 2006). To accommodate juvenile vulnerability and the accompanying need for protection, juvenile justice systems were introduced around the world (Oberlander, Goldstein, & Ho, 2001). Moreover, various jurisdictions around the world have introduced specific procedural safeguards attempting to counteract the effects of juveniles' developmental vulnerabilities (e.g., right to legal advice, attendance of appropriate adults; Quinn & Jackson, 2007). Nonetheless, those in direct contact with, and interviewing, juvenile suspects have an important role in ensuring appropriate strategies are employed.

In this chapter, specific concerns when interviewing juvenile suspects, such as suggestibility, not understanding their rights, and self-incrimination will be discussed. These sections will be followed by considerations when interviewing juvenile suspects, a case study, and recommendations to standard interview practices.

Implications for interviews

As mentioned above, it is surprising how little research is available on interviewing juvenile suspects (Redlich et al., 2004). This is especially the case given juvenile suspects' susceptibility to interrogative suggestibility, and subsequent false confessions (Cleary, 2014; Feld, 2006; Meyer & Reppucci, 2007). In contrast, there is ample research on how to interview child witnesses and victims (Winerdal et al., 2019). In general, research on interviewing child witnesses shows that suggestibility decreases with age (i.e., children are more suggestible than adults); compliance with authority plays a bigger role in children's interviews than adults; and when leading or suggestive questions are used, children are more likely to go along with these suggestions and provide inaccurate statements—especially when these questions are repeated (Meyer & Reppucci, 2007). However, in Chapter 6, we cannot simply apply findings from (child) witness research to (child) suspect cases. There are too many situational differences between juvenile suspects and victims (e.g., being accused of wrongdoing vs not; being interviewed about own actions vs someone else's actions; being cautioned or not; Winerdal et al., 2019), which impact the ability of the research to be transferred between the two.

The PEACE model has been found to be suitable for interviews with juveniles, but adjustments need to be made. Winerdal and colleagues (2019) evaluated the question types used in Swedish police interviews with young suspects of serious crimes. They started off by outlining that while special interviewing protocols were developed for interviewing child witnesses, this was not the case for juvenile suspects. Rather Swedish police officers needed to ensure that interviews with juvenile suspects should be conducted by police officers with a particular aptitude and to ensure that the potential for harm is minimised.

Suggestibility

One of the main concerns regarding juvenile suspects is that there may be heightened susceptibility to suggestion. Suggestibility refers to the inclination to accept suggestions provided by another person. These suggestions can be provided using leading questions, suggestive prompts, or (overt and covert) pressure during police interviews (Gudjonsson et al., 2016), and are more likely to be accepted during longer and/or repeated interviews (Kassin et al., 2010).

When referring specifically to suggestibility induced during interrogations, the term "interrogative suggestibility" is used (Meyer & Reppucci, 2007). Certain questions—such as those containing multiple parts, double negatives, and difficult vocabulary—increase suggestibility and thus inaccurate reports by juveniles (Meyer & Reppucci, 2007). Research has shown that juveniles in general are more suggestible than adults (Richardson, Gudjonsson, & Kelly, 1995), and that increased suggestibility during interviews not only increases inaccurate reports, but also the likelihood of false confessions (Meyer & Reppucci, 2007). As such, juvenile suspects are in a precarious position when being interviewed by police officers, as they are more vulnerable than adult suspects to interrogative pressure, and thus to falsely confessing (Cleary, 2014; Feld, 2006; Meyer & Reppucci, 2007).

It is not just suggestive questions though that contribute to interrogative suggestibility in juvenile suspects. Specific interviewing techniques that target the underdeveloped mental and/or social capacities in juveniles are effective in increasing suggestibility and thus false confessions (Feld, 2006). Police officers' use of children's eagerness to please; their respect and trust in authorities; the social expectancy of obedience; and their lower social status may increase suggestibility of children during interviews (Feld, 2006). Notably, suggestibility has not only been linked to false confessions, Redlich and colleagues (2003) showed that suggestibility was also linked to a decreased understanding of *Miranda* rights (i.e., cautions given to suspects).

Waiving rights

Cautions might be named differently around the world (e.g., "Miranda rights" in the United States), but they mostly cover similar rights: the right to remain silent (prevent self-incrimination) and a right to legal counsel. For a police interview to proceed in the United States a suspect must waive their rights. However, for this waiver to be accepted in court it must be made "knowingly, intelligently, and voluntarily" (Goldstein et al., 2003; Redlich et al., 2004). This implies that to be able to *legally* waive your rights you need to be able to understand what these rights actually mean (Abramovitch et al., 1993). Research shows that juveniles do not understand the function, and as such the importance, of their rights. Specifically, while they might understand that waiving their rights means they cannot have a person (or lawyer) present during their interview, younger juveniles in particular do not comprehend what the role of this person is within the interview process in the first place (Abramovitch et al., 1993; Feld, 2006).

It is, however, not just the understanding of Miranda rights that is impaired in juveniles. Redlich and colleagues (2004) reported that juveniles had far worse understanding of legal concepts in general than adults. Specifically, they reported that 11- to 15-year-old prisoners understood less of legal terms, and legal reasoning, than 16- to 17-year-olds and adults. Relatedly, Viljoen et al. (2005) found that younger adolescents (<15 years of age) were more likely to waive their right to counsel than older adolescents (15–17 years of age). Importantly, they further found that in contrast to older adolescents, younger adolescents' legal decisions (e.g., confess, plead guilty) were not predicted by the strength of evidence against them. As Feld (2006) stated: "generic developmental aspects of adolescents impair their ability to understand legal proceedings, to make rational decisions, or to assist counsel" (p. 232). This can result in juveniles being more likely to waive their rights (Abramovitch et al., 1993; Feld, 2006), and thus increasing their vulnerability and the risk of self-incrimination.

Self-incrimination

By waiving their rights, juveniles might increase their chances of self-incrimination, either resulting in a true or false confession. Research in general shows that younger children are more likely to self-incriminate than older children. This can be due to a lack of understanding that certain behaviours are actually crimes. For example, Billings et al. (2007) found that limited cognitive abilities and the lack of life experience meant that kindergarten children were unaware that admitting to guilty knowledge of a stealing actually incriminated them. Similarly, Redlich and Goodman (2003) found that age and suggestibility predicted self-incrimination. Twelve- and 13-year-olds, and those more suggestible, were more likely to take responsibility for a transgression than 15- to 16-year-olds, young adults, and those less suggestible, even when not guilty. There are other characteristics that make juveniles more likely to incriminate themselves and more likely to falsely confess. These factors include (but are not limited to) socio-economic status, low intelligence (with juvenile suspects having a lower Intelligence Quotient on average then their non-offending counterparts), and psychological disorders such as Attention Deficit Hyperactivity Disorder and Conduct Disorder (Gudjonson et al., 2016).

Interview guidelines

The interviewing of juvenile suspects has to be planned very carefully. Whatever steps are taken in order to ensure compliance with legislation and process will be subject to close scrutiny. This includes potential challenges to any assumptions as to the understanding made by interviewers as to the suspect's preparedness and ability to understand their situation. This includes associated legal issues and the consequences of any statements made by the suspect during the interview.

Many juvenile suspects are open to suggestibility and thus the framing of questions must be carefully considered. Agreeing with the interviewer may be a stance taken by the suspect if they feel that by doing so the interviewer will like them. Interview language should be in a format that is easily understood by the juvenile suspect. For example, "Tell the truth" statement may be explained in language, such as:

- being honest;
- not telling lies;
- only talking about things that really happened;
- things the suspect saw, heard, felt, smelt, touched;
- not making things up;
- not guessing.

It is important not to make assumptions about juvenile suspects. For example:

- the child has experience within the criminal justice process and is therefore less vulnerable;
- the parent or other family member/friend is the most Appropriate Adult to support the juvenile suspect;
- levels of understanding are on a par with the interviewer (particularly with older children and adolescents);
- I "know" the suspect therefore I will deal with them as I've always done;
- the suspect is experiencing their first time in custody so the interview will be easier.

The interviewer has to be prepared to provide a rationale for their approach and demonstrate that all reasonable steps have been taken to ensure fairness. Interviewers need to be self-aware of any attendant prejudice held by them surrounding social, behavioural, racial, and any impressions formed of the suspect through any previous dealings. It is the case that recidivism amongst some child offenders is high and thus there is already an established familiarity between the interviewing officer and the suspect. This is particularly the case in those police areas that are geographically smaller than others and where the "usual suspects" are familiar to the police in that area.

It is necessary that any safeguarding issues are not only considered but also seen to be addressed. All interactions with other relevant professionals need to be recorded, including:

- social workers;
- lawyers;
- interpreters;
- education;
- health professionals;
- family;
- other law enforcement agencies.

Undertaking thorough recording will ensure the requisite transparency. Recording should include not only the legal and procedural considerations but also those actions deemed to be appropriate for the interviewing of the particular suspect in the particular context rather than taking a routine approach simply to comply with procedures. These include:

- Timing of the interview to ensure that the interests of justice and the vulnerability of the suspect are protected. In some cases, and where the need for the interview is not time critical, interviewing officers should consider deferring the interview until more appropriate conditions can be achieved.
- How the interview is to be conducted. For example, if face-to-face video recording is appropriate or if the use of virtual interviewing is more appropriate.
- Location of the interview to engender an environment where the suspect feels less vulnerable and thus provide a greater opportunity for a meaningful interview.
- Persons present. If possible, agreement should be reached with representatives of the suspect to limit the number of people in the interview room which, in itself, can impact on the suspect's vulnerability. In some cases, the attendance of specialists identified to assist the suspect can actually achieve the opposite effect. In extreme cases the numbers can be inhibiting to the process and great care should be taken to ensure that only those essential individuals are present if fairness to the suspect is to be maintained.
- The identity of the interviewing officer in terms of prior knowledge of the suspect, gender, and age should be carefully calculated so that, where possible, the most appropriate individual(s) carry out the interview. This may not be the interviewer trained to the highest level but more the individual who has the better rapport and chemistry with the suspect.

Case study

Even though research and official guidelines for interviewing juvenile suspects are mostly absent (not just in Sweden but worldwide; Winerdal et al., 2019), in the United Kingdom (UK) safeguards have been introduced to protect vulnerable suspects during interviews and these apply to adults and juveniles. These safeguards include the right to access legal advice and an Appropriate Adult (AA; Pierpoint, 2000; Quinn & Jackson, 2007). The rationale for these safeguards is that juvenile suspects would be less likely to incriminate themselves, more confident during the police interview, and their statements would be more reliable. Careful choice of an Appropriate Adult (AA) should be made. The person deployed in that role should be selected having considered all of the attendant circumstances and who can best represent the suspect in relation to their vulnerability. Ideally, the Appropriate Adult should be a parent, guardian, or family member (however, if unsuitable or unavailable a social worker or lawyer could step in; Pierpoint, 2000). The role should only be determined with the best interests of the suspect in mind. The *Police and Criminal Evidence Act 1984* (UK) outlines that the AA should play an active role, advising the juvenile, making sure the interview is fair, and assisting the suspect with communication if needed (Quinn & Jackson, 2007). However, various researchers have found that Appropriate Adults often do not fulfil the role they are supposed to do (Pierpoint, 2000; Redlich et al., 2004; Woolard et al., 2008). Specifically, when the AA was a parent, their attendance during an interview could have a detrimental effect on the juvenile's interview (Redlich et al., 2004). Moreover, there may, of course, be circumstances in which certain facts may be revealed by the suspect that they would not wish to become known to a person with whom they have a close relationship. When it comes to cultural, language, and contemporary issues affecting children, not least the influence of relationships with peers, a person with a better understanding of the context of the situation of the suspect would be the most appropriate person. This includes the intellectual capability of the AA to be able to understand the requirement has to be considered if the vulnerability of the suspect is not to be aggravated. Professional AAs have been introduced but have been shown to only be effective if properly selected and prepared (Pierpoint, 2011; see Chapter 3 for further discussion of the role of third parties in interviews).

Conclusion

Juvenile suspects are especially vulnerable when it comes to being interviewed. Both impairments (due to age) in their social and cognitive abilities place juveniles at risk of unfair judicial outcomes. Juveniles are socially vulnerable in interviews as they commonly have an eagerness to please, especially those in authority positions. Moreover, their own lower social status during interviews in combination with trust in authorities increases the possibility that they will go along with whatever the interviewer says. The increased susceptibility to (interrogative) suggestibility not only increases the chances of juveniles to self-incriminate by waiving their rights, going along with suggestions during interviews can lead to false confessions as well.

However, accommodations can be made for these vulnerabilities. Firstly, proper interview guidelines should be used. The above provided guidelines in combination with the PEACE model can protect children against their own vulnerabilities to some extent. Ideally, an AA or support person should also sit in with the juvenile and support them both emotionally and cognitively. While parents are often the first point of contact when a juvenile is arrested, considerations should be made regarding who would be the best person to support the child. Following these adjustments will provide some safeguards when interviewing a juvenile suspect and as such increase the fairness of the process.

References

Abramovitch, R., Higgins-Biss, K.L., & Biss, S.R. (1993). Young persons' comprehension of waivers in criminal proceedings. *Canadian Journal of Criminology, 35*(3), 309–321.

Billings, F.J., Taylor, T., Burns, J., Corey, D.L., Garven, S., & Wood, J.M. (2007). Can reinforcement induce children to falsely incriminate themselves?. *Law and Human Behavior, 31*(2), 125–139.

Cleary, H. (2014). Police interviewing and interrogation of juvenile suspects: A descriptive examination of actual cases. *Law and Human Behavior, 38*(3), 271.

Feld, B.C. (2006). Police interrogation of juveniles: An empirical study of policy and practice. *Journal of Criminal Law and Criminology, 97*, 219.

Goldstein, N.E.S., Condie, L.O., Kalbeitzer, R., Osman, D., & Geier, J.L. (2003). Juvenile offenders' Miranda rights comprehension and self-reported likelihood of offering false confessions. *Assessment, 10*(4), 359–369.

Gross, S.R., Jacoby, K., Matheson, D.J., Montgomery, N., & Patil, S. Exonerations in the United States 1989 through 2003'(2005). *Journal of Criminal Law and Criminology, 95*, 523.

Gudjonsson, G.H., Sigurdsson, J.F., Sigfusdottir, I.D., Asgeirsdottir, B.B., González, R.A., & Young, S. (2016). A national epidemiological study investigating risk factors for police interrogation and false confession among juveniles and young persons. *Social Psychiatry and Psychiatric Epidemiology, 51*(3), 359–367.

Kassin, S.M., Drizin, S.A., Grisso, T., Gudjonsson, G.H., Leo, R.A., & Redlich, A.D. (2010). Police-induced confessions: Risk factors and recommendations. *Law and Human Behavior, 34*(1), 3–38.

Malloy, L.C., Shulman, E.P., & Cauffman, E. (2014). Interrogations, confessions, and guilty pleas among serious adolescent offenders. *Law and Human Behavior, 38*(2), 181.

Meyer, J.R., & Reppucci, N.D. (2007). Police practices and perceptions regarding juvenile interrogation and interrogative suggestibility. *Behavioral Sciences & the Law, 25*(6), 757–780.

Oberlander, L.B., Goldstein, N.E., & Ho, C.N. (2001). Preadolescent adjudicative competence: Methodological considerations and recommendations for practice standards. *Behavioral Sciences & the Law, 19*(4), 545–563.

Pierpoint, H. (2000). How appropriate are volunteers as' appropriate adults' for young suspects? The'appropriate adult'system and human rights. *The Journal of Social Welfare & Family Law, 22*(4), 383–400.

Pierpoint, H. (2011). Extending and professionalising the role of the appropriate adult. *Journal of Social Welfare and Family Law, 33*(2), 139–155.

Quinn, K., & Jackson, J. (2007). Of rights and roles: Police interviews with young suspects in Northern Ireland. *British Journal of Criminology, 47*(2), 234–255.

Redlich, A.D., & Goodman, G.S. (2003). Taking responsibility for an act not committed: The influence of age and suggestibility. *Law and Human Behavior, 27*(2), 141–156.

Redlich, A.D., Silverman, M., Chen, J., & Steiner, H. (2004). The police interrogation of children and adolescents. In *Interrogations, confessions, and entrapment* (pp. 107–125). Springer.

Redlich, A.D., Ghetti, S., & Quas, J.A. (2008). Perceptions of children during a police interview: A comparison of alleged victims and suspects 1. *Journal of Applied Social Psychology, 38*(3), 705–735.

Richardson, G., Gudjonsson, G.H., & Kelly, T.P. (1995). Interrogative suggestibility in an adolescent forensic population. *Journal of Adolescence, 18*(2), 211–216.

Viljoen, J.L., Klaver, J., & Roesch, R. (2005). Legal decisions of preadolescent and adolescent defendants: Predictors of confessions, pleas, communication with attorneys, and appeals. *Law and Human Behavior, 29*(3), 253–277.

Winerdal, U., Cederborg, A.C., & Lindholm, J. (2019). The quality of question types in Swedish police interviews with young suspects of serious crimes. *The Police Journal, 92*(2), 136–149.

Woolard, J.L., Cleary, H., Harvell, S.A., & Chen, R. (2008). Examining adolescents' and their parents' conceptual and practical knowledge of police interrogation: A family dyad approach. *Journal of Youth and Adolescence, 37*(6), 685–698.

Chapter 9

Interviewing suspects with mental illness

Jane Tudor-Owen, Celine van Golde, and David Gee

Executive summary

Psychological vulnerability can be hard to detect as it is largely invisible. There are exceptions to this; for example, a person experiencing a psychotic episode, but these are less common. Once psychological vulnerability has been identified, either through questioning, screening, or specific behaviours, it is important to carefully plan the interview. As previously discussed, formalised interview plans may assist in turning your attention to key areas to consider.

The particular concern for interviews conducted with people with mental illness is the risk they do not understand their rights or the implications of waiving them, and the risk of false confessions (Amos, 2021). Fortunately, investigative interviewing models, for example, PEACE, have inbuilt features to minimise these risks. In responding to people with mental illness in crisis, policing agencies around the world are moving towards specialist units with targeted training for first responders. The success of these operations suggests specialist mental health training for police interviewers may be one option to safeguard the process for suspects with psychological vulnerabilities.

This chapter contains a discussion of perceptions held by police and people with mental illness, implications for interviewing, and a case study to consider contemporary ways of working with suspects who are psychologically vulnerable.

Introduction

In recent times the opportunity to interview suspects has been impacted by the significant increase in suspects identified as experiencing mental illness. Living with a mental illness does not necessarily mean there is a psychological vulnerability, depending on how the mental illness is managed. However, there are circumstances where the illness has not been managed and symptoms may therefore increase vulnerability. It is what to do in these circumstances that the remainder of the present chapter is concerned with. The legal implications are significant, for example, when assessing fitness for interview, fitness to plead, and moral culpability. What makes matters more complex is the inherently dynamic nature of many mental illnesses and the way in which they may impact cognition and/or behaviour, meaning there is no "one-size-fits-all" approach even with respect to any one individual.

Encounters between police and people with mental illness pose significant risk for all parties (Kerr et al., 2010). When there are incidents involving police response to mental health crises that end in physical injury, these are widely reported. However, as is often the case with police publicity, the many responses that are resolved with positive outcomes are not reported. As a result, there is likely to be a misrepresentation of both people with mental illness in the community and police responses to crisis calls.

DOI: 10.4324/9781003145998-12

Chapter 2 of this book addresses how vulnerability might be identified by police officers. The present chapter deals specifically with people with mental illness who have a particular kind of psychological vulnerability. This population is often difficult for police to identify as the vulnerability is typically not visible (Herrington & Roberts, 2012) and it is important to identify as early as possible (Gudjonsson, 2010). Further, the nature of the vulnerability, depending on the specific characteristics of the mental illness, can pose difficulties for information processing and communication (Gudjonsson, 2010; Herrington & Roberts, 2012). In addition to the challenges in obtaining reliable information from some suspects with a mental illness, psychological vulnerability may also explain behaviours that would otherwise be unexpected (Amos, 2021; Herrington & Roberts, 2012; Lipson et al., 2010). For example, the suspect may excessively fidget, sweat, or be speaking to someone who is not in the room. It is important to note here that while there are challenges, this does not mean that suspects with a mental illness are not able to provide reliable information (Gudjonsson, 2010); rather, the onus is on the agency, and the interviewers, to be mindful of the way in which the suspect may be more vulnerable and research has shown that police are able to inform themselves with regard to potential psychological vulnerabilities using intelligence provided at dispatch, from people known to the suspect, and from their own observations (Bohrman et al., 2018).

In this chapter, perceptions of people with mental illness will be discussed, followed by implications for interviewing including screening and false confessions. These sections will be followed by recommended modifications to standard interviewing practices and a case study considering contemporary approaches to engaging with suspects experiencing mental illness.

Perceptions of police held by people with mental illness

Researchers have analysed the perceptions held by people with a mental illness in regard to their interactions with police. In Canada, researchers found that while the sample had frequent interactions with police, 72% were satisfied with how police handled the most recent interaction and the majority believed it to be procedurally just (Livingstone, Desmarais, Verdun-Jones, Parent, Michalak, & Brink, 2014). In terms of previous experiences, 32% of the sample indicated that their previous interactions were negative. Participants in that study noted the importance of the police finding the right people for the job, suggesting the need for either specialised training and/or a specific skill set for successfully working with people with a mental illness. In particular, they noted the need for effective and compassionate communication (Livingstone, Desmarais, Verdun-Jones, Parent, Michalak, & Brink, 2014).

Perceptions of procedural justice can be influenced by a number of factors, and these can be specific to the population. Understanding what specific factors are relevant to the population you are working with is essential to ensuring they perceive themselves to have been treated in a procedurally just manner. In a study examining perceptions of procedural justice by people with mental illness, findings showed that police interactions that had involved threats, physical force, deception, coercion, and arrest or apprehension were perceived as less procedurally just (Livingston et al., 2014). In those circumstances, perceptions of procedural justice are going to be influenced by the outcome potentially more than the manner in which it came about. In that study, participants reported higher perceived procedural justice concerning interactions that occurred when they were experiencing a mental health crisis, than in other police interactions. Ultimately, the findings suggested that police adopting a cooperative approach are more likely to be perceived as procedurally just.

Implications for interviews

Screening for mental illness

Screening detainees is understandably a difficult process as, unless it is routine, it requires police to first identify an individual as being potentially vulnerable. Screening tools have been developed in response to concerns that practices police have historically adopted under-identify people with mental illness who may benefit from tailored approaches to detention, including investigative procedures like interviewing (Baksheev et al., 2012). However, in respect to the sample of 150 detainees in two metropolitan police stations in Melbourne, Australia, use of standardised screening tools was found to be more accurate in identifying mental illness in detainees than non-standardised health screens which included questions about mental health (Baksheev et al., 2012).

The Brief Jail Mental Health Screen has been used internationally to screen detainees. Dorn et al. (2013) surveyed Police Service Amsterdam-Amstelland detainees in the Netherlands and found that 40% of the 264 randomly selected detainees obtained a score indicating further evaluation was warranted. In Baksheev and colleagues' (2012) sample of 132 detainees, 58.3% were assessed as requiring further evaluation. Routine screening provides a measure of security in ensuring that people who require additional assistance due to their specific vulnerability are afforded those safeguards, but it is far from perfect. It also provides the opportunity to refer those individuals for assistance outside the criminal justice system, ideally avoiding future interactions with that system (Dorn et al., 2013).

The absence of reliable screening has implications for people with mental illness, but also for the justice system more broadly, particularly when evidence is obtained under circumstances where a suspect's vulnerability is not accounted for. It is vital in terms of guarding against wrongful conviction that evidence is obtained lawfully; however, there can be devastating implications when a guilty suspect cannot be prosecuted due to the manner in which evidence of their guilt has been obtained. When the stakes are high, for example in cases of violent and sexual offences, this is particularly so. Clugston and colleagues (2019) reviewed 31 interviews with people with mental illness who were charged with murder or attempted murder in Queensland, Australia. Symptoms of mental illness were identified in all interviews, ranging from pervasive to seldom in frequency. A support person was present in three of the interviews but there were no interviews where a legal practitioner was present. In terms of attempting to identify concerns around vulnerability within the interview, police officers asked about substance use (74.2%) more often than mental illness (58.1%). Encouraging the presence of support people and legal practitioners in interviewing with suspects with mental illness is an unambiguous way to safeguard the interview process, particularly when the suspect is being interviewed in relation to a serious offence (Clugston et al., 2019). In Clugston and colleagues' (2019) study, there was some concern around the reluctance of police to end the interview when requested. This is unlikely to be as much of an issue when there are third parties present.

While training police is always important, it is imperative to remember that police are not mental health professionals. Contrary to expectation, in early research examining the impact of Crisis Intervention Team (CIT) training, Kerr and colleagues (2010) found training did not reduce the likelihood of injuries in callouts involving people with mental illness; however, analyses showed use of force affected level of resistance posed by people with mental illness which in turn increased the likelihood of injury to people with a mental illness (Kerr et al., 2010), highlighting that skills in de-escalation are likely to be of the most benefit in all but the most serious of circumstances. People with mental illness who were asked about their experiences indicated that police training needed to include the following core areas: understanding mental illness and its effects; communicating effectively; treating people with compassion; and prioritising non-violent responses (Livingstone et al., 2014). More recent research examining the effect of CIT training found that CIT-trained officers responding to mental health crisis calls spent significantly more time with the person with a mental illness and asked more questions of the individual (Felix-Ortiz et al., 2021). These findings show the benefits that can be realised through targeted training for specialised units.

False confessions

One of the key concerns when interviewing suspects with mental illness is the increased risk of false confessions or admissions against interest. This risk is exacerbated by circumstances in which the suspect does not fully understand the implications for such statements and/or does not understand their rights including, relevantly, the right to silence. Volbert and colleagues (2019) surveyed forensic patients in Germany about their interview experiences with police and found that all participants had been interviewed when guilty, and 62% had been interviewed when innocent. Of those participants who were interviewed when innocent, 25% reported falsely confessing on at least one occasion. Concerningly, 15 of the 24 participants who reported falsely confessing were later convicted (Volbert et al., 2019). Characteristics of interviews with people with mental illness where false confessions were obtained as opposed to true confessions include increased numbers of interviews, longer periods of time in the interview until confession, and evidence was perceived by the person with mental illness as comparatively weaker (Redlich et al., 2011). In that study, the researchers found false confessors (who had mostly also truly confessed on occasion) reported more external pressure and less internal pressure than true confessors. In terms of demographic characteristics, there were no significant differences with regard to ethnicity, age, education, diagnosis, or criminality. Implications of these findings include the need to limit the number of times people with mental illness are interviewed about the same offending and to ensure that any admissions are corroborated.

People with mental illness who falsely confess do so for different reasons than those who truly confess. False confessions were mostly likely to protect someone (29%), due to perceived leniency (23%), and perceived threat (19%; Redlich et al., 2011). The latter two reasons are most concerning as, with regard to leniency, depending on the ability of the person to stand trial, or the defence raised, they may be detained indefinitely if they are deemed without capacity. With regard to threat, this is also likely to be a factor to which people with particular forms of mental illness are more vulnerable to experiencing (i.e., mental illness with paranoid features).

Early identification, interview techniques, and ensuring safeguards are in place provide the best opportunity for people with mental illness to be interviewed in such a way as to minimise the risk of their being placed at a disadvantage due to their specific vulnerability (Clugston et al., 2019; Gudjonsson, 2010). While helpful, screening is not necessarily the answer, as it is likely to identify the need for treatment, rather than providing information regarding capacity to understand what is occurring (Clugston et al., 2019).

Interview guidelines

- Prior to the interview, observe the suspect and their interactions with others, and be ready to request a psychological evaluation if there is doubt of their capacity to engage in an interview (Herrington & Roberts, 2012).
- The presence of a trained Appropriate Adult (Herrington & Roberts, 2012).
- Ensure the suspect understands their rights (Herrington & Roberts, 2012); for example, by asking them to summarise them in their own words.

- Maintain a calm environment, including the demeanour of the interviewers (Herrington & Roberts, 2012).
- Take regular breaks.
- Adopt "suspended belief" with individuals whose actions are on the basis of delusional thinking (Lipson et al., 2010). This approach requires the other party, in this context it would be police, to communicate to the person with mental illness that you are aware that the individual has a belief that explains their actions, you will listen to their explanation, but that you are also obliged to source additional information to corroborate their explanation.

Case study

Most police forces throughout England and Wales together with local National Health Service partners have since introduced what are known as Liaison and Diversion (LD) teams within custody suites to assist in the identification of any mental illness being suffered by suspects prior to interview.

One such unit is working effectively within the police custody suite based in Middlesbrough in the northeast of England. The team aims to "screen" all suspects prior to interview and often achieves that goal, dependent on volume of persons arrested at peak times. The LD team operates within the custody suite during the hours of 8am and 8pm daily.

The flow of the procedure is:

1. suspect arrives in Custody Suite;
2. if Custody Officer authorises detention of Suspect;
3. details forwarded to SPECTRUM (police intelligence team) to identify any intelligence available as to capacity of suspect to be interviewed;
4. SPECTRUM results to Liaison and Diversion (LD) team;
5. suspect assessed by LD team for any requirement of Appropriate Adult (AA);
6. if decision is that an AA is required the MIND (mental health charity) on-call volunteer is called to assist suspect throughout the interview.

The team estimates that some 50% of overall suspects are suffering from the effects of some form of mental illness within a total throughput of 16,000 detainees per year. This includes any temporary incapacity through the effects of drugs and other medication as well as those suspects suffering from an identified mental health condition, either pre-diagnosed or not. This volume places a significant burden on the team and the investigating officers to ensure that the requirements of Code C are met and that the wellbeing of the suspect is ensured.

The requirement for LD intervention is where there is previously held intelligence within the SPECTRUM database surrounding any recorded mental health issues relating to the suspect. There is a similar requirement in those cases where any concerns are expressed by the arresting officer and/or the Custody Officer as to the ability of the suspect to be able to have sufficient understanding of the interview process. In Middlesbrough, the procedure goes one step further and actually screens every suspect detained for interview notwithstanding any concerns raised in order to ensure absolute fairness to the suspect. Given the propensity of increased drug misuse and the combined effects of alcohol, prescribed and over-the-counter medication, this additional measure seems to be most appropriate but is obviously resource intensive.

Where the LD team forms the view that the suspect would benefit from support and guidance from an AA during any interview, the on-call MIND volunteer is called and attends the interview as required. This procedure enjoys the participation and cooperation of each agency involved given the potential for tensions between investigators and NHS LD teams. Anecdotally, it has been observed that any initial mistrust of the procedure has been eliminated with all participants observing absolute fairness to the suspect prior to and during the interview process. This is additional to the existing provisions within the *PACE Act* surrounding legal representation. It does not prohibit interview of the suspect in extremis, i.e., where failure to do so would put life at risk, but seeks to strike a balance in terms of safeguarding the process and ensuring protection of life.

Conclusion

Interviewing a suspect with either a known or suspected mental illness can be daunting, particularly when the stakes are high. Specialised training is one way of increasing both skill and confidence, but it is important to remember that following the investigative interviewing approach with reasonable modifications as outlined above will provide police with the opportunity to interview the suspect while ensuring fairness in that process.

In many jurisdictions around the world, police enjoy the benefit of electronically recorded interviews and body-worn cameras. In interactions with vulnerable suspects, these are of particular importance to both police and suspects. These recordings provide evidence of the manner in which a vulnerable suspect has been dealt with, reassuring prosecutors, defence counsel, judicial officers, and juries that the process has been safeguarded. To that end, police should encourage third parties to attend where appropriate as it further demonstrates fairness and can provide assistance in communicating with the suspect. Finally, there is no substitute for carefully thought-out interview planning, including with respect to appropriate language, checking the caution, and the provision of breaks. Planning for multiple eventualities will provide interviewers with the greatest flexibility, maximising the prospects of an investigatively useful interview.

References

Amos, L. (2021). Wrongful convictions and mental illness: A qualitative case-study of James Blackmon. *Wrongful Conviction Law Review, 2*, 22–54.

Baksheev, G.N., Ogloff, J., & Thomas, S. (2012). Identification of mental illness in police cells: A comparison of police processes, the brief jail mental health screen and the jail screening assessment tool. *Psychology, Crime & Law, 18*(6), 529–542. doi: 10.1080/1068316X.2010.510118

Bohrman, C., Blank Wilson, A., Watson, A., & Draine, J. (2018). How police officers assess for mental illnesses. *Victims & Offenders, 13*(8), 1077–1092.

Clugston, B., Green, B., Phillips, J., Samaraweera, Z., Ceron, C., Gardner, C., Meurk, C., Heffernan, E. (2019). Interviewing persons with mental illness charged with murder or attempted murder: A retrospective review of police interviews. *Psychiatry, Psychology and Law, 26*(6), 904–919. doi: 10.1080/13218719.2019.1642260

Dorn, T., Ceelen, M., Buster, M., & Das, K. (2013). Screening for mental illness among persons in Amsterdam Police custody. *Psychiatric Services, 64*(10), 1047–1050.

Felix-Ortiz, M., Steele, C., DeGuzman, M., Guerrero, G., Graham, M. (2021). A participatory action research study of police interviewing following crisis intervention team training. *Verbum Incarnatum: An Academic Journal of Social Justice, 8*, Article 2. Retrieved from https://athenaeum.uiw.edu/cgi/viewcontent.cgi?article=1075&context=verbumincarnatum

Gudjonsson, G.H. (2010). Psychological vulnerabilities during police interviews. Why are they important? *Legal and Criminological Psychology, 15*, 161–175. doi: 10.1348/135532510X500064

Herrington, V., & Roberts, K. (2012). Addressing psychology vulnerability in the police suspect interview. *Policing, 6*(2), 177–186. doi: 10.1093/police/par057

Kerr, A.N, Morabito, M., Watson, A.C. (2010). Police encounters, mental illness, and injury: An exploratory investigation. *Journal of Police Crisis Negotiations, 10*, 116–132. doi: 10.1080/15332581003757198

Lipson, G.S, Turner, J.T., & Kasper, R. (2010). A strategic approach to police interactions involving persons with mental illness. *Journal of Police Crisis Negotiations, 10*, 30–38. doi: 10.1080/15332581003757297

Livingston, J.D., Desmarais, S.L., Verdun-Jones, S., Parent, R., Michalak, E., & Brink, J. (2014). Perceptions and experiences of people with mental illness regarding their interactions with police. *International Journal of Law and Psychiatry, 37*, 334–340. doi: 10.1016/j.ijlp.2014.02.003

Redlich, A.D., Kulish, R., & Steadman, H.J. (2011). Comparing true and false confessions among persons with serious mental illness. *Psychology, Public Policy and Law, 17*(3), 394–418. doi: 10.1037/a0022918

Volbert, R., May, L., Hausam, J., & Lau, S. (2019). Confessions and denials when guilty and innocent: Forensic patients' self-reported behaviour during police interviews. *Frontiers in Psychiatry, 10*, 168–177. doi: 10.3389/fpsyt.2019.00168

Chapter 10

Interviewing suspects with intellectual and learning impairments

Celine van Golde, Jane Tudor-Owen and David Gee

Executive summary

There are various disorders that are often mentioned under the same moniker as intellectual and learning disorders, such as Foetal Alcohol Spectrum Disorder (FASD) and Autism Spectrum Disorder (ASD). However, these disorders are distinct. People with these disorders might experience similar (but not identical) impairments of their intellectual and learning abilities. Nevertheless, each disorder causes different patterns of impairments which will affect suspects with these disorders in different ways during interviews.

Accommodations can be made for these suspects and will differ based on the specific impairments experienced. In general, suggestibility, compliance, and understanding questions are difficult for suspects with Intellectual Disabilities (ID), FASD, or ASD, and will affect the quality of the information provided and the integrity of the interview. This chapter will outline each disorder separately in terms of what it is, its prevalence, and how it impacts interviews. Lastly, guidelines for interviewing suspects with these disorders will be provided for each separately.

Introduction

Intellectual and learning impairments impact cognitive functioning (e.g., memory, inhibition, problem-solving), communication, but may also impact social abilities and self-care skills (Murphy & Clare, 1998). Within the general population the prevalence of Intellectual Disabilities (ID) is not high (Henshaw et al., 2018; Mogavero, 2020); however, when we look at the prevalence of people with ID in the criminal justice system, we see another picture. There is a vast overrepresentation of both victims and offenders with ID (Henshaw et al., 2018). For example, in the United States prison population, an approximate 19.5% of inmates reportedly has a cognitive disability (Mogavero, 2020), compared to 4.8% in the general population (Bronson, Maruschak, & Berzofsky, 2015). Australian and international data show similar rates with up to 15% of prisoners being diagnosed with an ID (compared to 2.9% prevalence in the general Australian population; Dowse et al., 2021). These rates are even higher for children (Chapter 8) and Indigenous Australians (Chapter 11). Moreover, people with an ID are more likely to suffer from various forms of social disadvantages such as poverty, violence, and homelessness (Dowse et al., 2021), demonstrating that offenders often have multiple vulnerabilities (Dowse et al., 2021). Looking at these statistics it becomes clear that while the presence of an ID might not predict offending behaviour, the social comorbidities that come with ID increase the possibilities of "over-policing". This in turn inflates the representation of people with ID in the criminal justice system (Dowse et al., 2021).

DOI: 10.4324/9781003145998-13

Intellectual Disabilities can be mild, moderate, severe, and profound. The extent of the disability determines the level of accommodation required in a suspect interview. Because people with mild ID can function independently in everyday life, their impairment is often not directly visible. However, their disability means that they need assistance in complex tasks, such as making decisions regarding their health and the law (Schatz, 2018). Individuals who are diagnosed with a moderate ID can be independent when it comes to personal care and living; however, they need extended training to be able to do this. Suspects with a mild or moderate ID are at risk during an interview, as their vulnerability might not be visible, and thus not identified and mitigated. Specifically, while officers can be understanding and accommodating towards those with an ID, this is hard when they cannot identify an ID is present (Schatz, 2018). Individuals with severe and profound ID will generally require continuous support for all activities they do and/or are completely dependent on caregivers. They often have extremely limited or non-existent language skills and as such are very unlikely to be interviewed as suspects (Schatz, 2018).

Criminal justice processes are cognitively demanding and require suspects to understand complicated concepts and terminology (such as cautions and charges). These expectations might be greatly misplaced for suspects with an ID, as their cognitive abilities and communications skills may be limited (Henshaw et al., 2018; Murphy & Clare, 1998). In turn, these deficiencies will impact the effectiveness of the interview. Suspects with limited communication skills might not understand the questions being asked, and just simply reply back using terms from the questions, appearing to talk about the same topic. At the same time, suspects with learning disabilities are inclined to comply with requests (even when not in their own best interest), especially when the requests are posed by an authority figure, such as a police officer (Murphy & Clare, 1998). Lastly, people with learning disabilities are likely to change their answers and confabulate details when being interviewed in a suggestive way, creating the impression that they change their stories (Murphy & Clare, 1998). These findings demonstrate how important it is to accommodate intellectual and learning disabilities in interviews.

This chapter will next focus on various impairments that impact intellectual, cognitive, and social functioning, namely Foetal Alcohol Spectrum Disorder (FASD) and Autism Spectrum Disorder (ASD). Definitions, prevalence, and methods of identification will be provided for each disorder. This is followed by a discussion on the impact these various disorders have (including ID) on interviewing practices for each disorder separately. Lastly, adaptations to interview guidelines will be provided.

Foetal Alcohol Spectrum Disorder

Foetal Alcohol Spectrum Disorder (FASD) is a neurodevelopmental disorder which impacts a wide variety of functions, such as cognitive functioning, the ability to communicate, and social and affective functioning. FASD is caused by the foetus being exposed to alcohol in the womb, which causes neural functional and structural abnormalities. The disorder will affect a person for their whole life. The severity and symptoms of the disorder vary widely, but can require lifelong support to accommodate the needs of the impairments experienced by the person with FASD (Brown, 2020; Mc Lachlan, 2021). Notably, the abilities impacted by FASD—impulsivity, gullibility, compliance, and suggestibility—create severe vulnerabilities in suspects with FASD during interviews (Alley & Mukherjee, 2019).

The prevalence of FASD is difficult to establish. It is notoriously underdiagnosed due to a lack of proper training in health professionals (Alley & Mukherjee, 2019). In the United States, it is speculated that between 1% and 5% of the population have FASD (Brown et al., 2020; McLachlan, 2021). However, when looking at the rest of the world, estimates of the prevalence of FASD differ substantially (McLachlan, 2021). There is an overrepresentation in the criminal justice system of victims and offenders with FASD. Brown et al. (2020) noted that people with FASD were 30 times more likely to get in contact with the criminal justice system and 19 times more likely to end up in jail compared to those who do not have the disorder. Moreover, it has been suggested that well over 50% of all people with FASD will be arrested for at least one crime (McLachlan, 2021).

FASD can be extremely difficult to identify as it is considered an "invisible" disability. Moreover, suspects can conceal some of the indicators that may be more obvious. For example, suspects with FASD have been found to effectively use verbal and social skills to hide the extent of their impairments (McLachlan, 2021). While police officers might report receiving no training aimed at identifying and working with suspects with FASD (Allely & Mukherjee, 2019), they are not alone. Allely and Mukherjee (2019) indicated that mental health professionals lack sufficient training in identifying FASD, and as such there is a chronic underdiagnosis of the disorder. This means that suspects may not be aware of the impairment and will therefore be unable to alert police.

Autism Spectrum Disorder

Autism Spectrum Disorder (ASD) is a neurodevelopmental disorder which manifests in the three forms of impairment: social communication, social interaction, and social imagination (Hepworth, 2017). It is a lifelong condition which often includes repetitive activities, behaviours, and interest (Maras et al., 2018). As the name—Autism *Spectrum* Disorder—suggests, there is a wide variety in the severity of symptoms and they manifest in individual diagnoses (Hepworth, 2017; Maras et al., 2018). Notably, ASD includes both Autism and what was previously known as Asperger's Syndrome. The number of people with an ASD diagnosis is steadily increasing. It was estimated that four or five children per 10,000 children had ASD in the UK in 2005 (Chown, 2010), while the Centers of Disease Control and Prevention stated that one in 54 children were diagnosed with ASD in the United States in 2016 (Christiansen et al., 2021). Hepworth (2017) estimated that one in 45 adults was diagnosed with ASD. Some people prefer the descriptor "neurodiverse" over ASD; however, for ease, and given that neurodiversity can refer to other neurological disorders (e.g., Attention Deficit Hyperactivity Disorder, ADHD), we will use the term ASD in this chapter.

While ASD organisations around the world state there is no link between ASD and criminal offending (Chown, 2010), this does not mean there is no contact with the criminal justice system. People with ASD are reportedly seven times more likely to come into contact with the criminal justice system than those without ASD (Christiansen, 2021). Christiansen and colleagues further stated that nearly 5% of juveniles with ASD had been arrested, while 20% had been stopped by the police at least once. These statistics are reflected in prison numbers where 5–40% of prisoners were diagnosed with ASD compared to 0.3–2% in the general population (Hepworth, 2017). It has been suggested that while there might be no direct link between ASD and criminal offending, interactions between ASD, social factors, and/or comorbidities with other impairments could be the reason for the high numbers reported (Chown, 2010). Moreover, ASD individuals presenting as "different", in contrast to those whose symptoms are less noticeable, could make them more visible to the police.

ASD is often classified as an "invisible disability" as there are no *immediately* visible symptoms non-experts can use for identification, although, as noted above, some people with ASD exhibit behaviours that make them more noticeable (Hepworth, 2017). In confirmation, 80% of US police officers participating in a study on "knowledge and perceptions of persons with disabilities" were unable to accurately provide a symptom of ASD. Of those officers,

35% provided "Rain man" as an answer when they were asked what the term Autism meant to them (Chown, 2010). This pop culture reference demonstrates the stereotypes held towards people with ASD. In contrast, it seems that personal experience (rather than pop culture knowledge) can help when trying to identify ASD. Christiansen and colleagues (2021) reported that officers who had personal experience with ASD were better able to indicate if someone had ASD in a vignette study, compared to those officers that lacked personal experience. However, when a suspect with ASD displayed subtle symptoms, both groups of officers—those with and without personal experience—struggled to identify that person as having ASD.

ASD is challenging for mental health professionals to identify, and it is therefore important to remember police are not trained in the diagnosis of mental disorders and it is not an expectation of their role. However, identifying ASD is essential for the integrity of any interview (Maras et al., 2018). In the UK it was proposed to put the onus partly back on the suspect. Specifically, the custody officer, when determining the welfare of the suspect, should include the question "Do you have any difficulties that I may not be aware of?" (Chown, 2010; Hepworth, 2017). This question is supposed to make the invisible disability visible. However, critics of this approach have pointed out that the custody suite in a police station might not be the best environment to openly disclose mental health disorders (Bradley, 2009). Maras et al. (2018) suggested that this hesitance to disclose could be overcome by making sure the person with ASD feels comfortable disclosing that information and understands that accommodations can be made (such as appointing an AA) once ASD has been identified. At the same time, people with ASD participating in a study on their perspectives of the custody process indicated that the pre-set question might not allow people to adequately disclose their diagnosis (Holloway et al.,2020). This can be because people with ASD might not consider ASD "a difficulty" for a variety of reasons which go beyond the scope of this chapter. However, if suspects with ASD do not disclose their impairment, their vulnerability can go unidentified by the interviewer. While this might not be a problem regarding the duty of care held towards suspects, it can impact the later admissibility of any admissions made during the preamble of the interview. One option is for the interviewer to ask an additional probative question; for example, do you have any mental illness or impairments? While the onus is still on the suspect to disclose, it is an explicit question in a more private setting than that afforded in a custody suite.

Implications for interviewing a suspect with ID

Police officers' awareness of the presence of ID affects the adjustments they make when interviewing vulnerable suspects. Police officers heavily rely on the communication skills and cognitive ability of suspects, both for administering the caution and conducting the interview. These abilities may be impaired for suspects with ID. As such, especially those with "non-obvious" disabilities will be impacted before and during police interviews if their vulnerability is not identified (Dowse et al., 2021; Henshaw et al., 2018). Studies have found that people with ID are less likely to understand their rights than those without an ID (Henshaw et al., 2018). Without proper understanding of these rights a person with an ID is more likely to incriminate themselves, while at the same time any evidence they provide in the interview can later be ruled inadmissible. Similarly, cognitive impairment affects understanding of the purpose of the interview and questions asked, and can impact how a suspect with an ID will respond. This becomes a problem when suspects just agree with questions, rephrase what is being said to them (echolalia), and go along with suggestions, which changes their account because they do not comprehend the purpose of an interview (Henshaw et al., 2018).

Not only will these behaviours make the suspect's statement seem unreliable, they will also hamper the integrity of the investigation. Moreover, it increases the chances of a suspect with an ID making a false confession (Schatz, 2018). Data on wrongful convictions have shown that especially those with ID (including ASD, FASD, and ADHD) are likely to get their convictions overturned (Dowse et al., 2021; Mogavero, 2020; Young et al., 2013). As such, early identification of these disabilities is of the utmost importance for the integrity of the judicial system.

Police officers often rely on self-identification of people with an impairment; however, this has been shown to be very unreliable and as such a vulnerable suspect will not get the support they need (Henshaw et al., 2018; Young et al., 2013). One of the accommodations that can be made to assist suspects with ID during interviews is the presence of an Appropriate Adult (AA; see also Chapter 3 for a discussion regarding third parties in interviews and Chapter 8 for a discussion of the use of AAs in interviews with suspects who are children). AAs are called upon when a suspect is identified as vulnerable due to age (juvenile suspect), mental health issues (Chapter 9), or as having an ID (Henshaw et al., 2018; Young et al., 2013). The main purpose of an AA is to provide advice and support during an interview; however, they can also assist before and after the interview has taken place. Some researchers have suggested that this role requires two people: one person to consider the legal safety of the suspect, while the other looks after their emotional safety (Henshaw et al., 2018).

Implications for interviewing a suspect with FASD

FASD can severely impact a suspect's access to justice. The impairments experienced by those with FASD can impact their ability to participate in all of the different stages of the criminal justice system. Waiving rights, understanding the purpose of an interview, (falsely) confessing, and understanding trial procedures are all impacted by FASD symptoms and can lead to wrongful convictions (Alley & Mukherjee, 2019; McLachlan, 2021). Given suspects with FASD often suffer from cognitive and communicative impairments, understanding their rights and being able to self-assess their understanding of these rights is affected. Moreover, providing a written version of their rights might also not be helpful, as suspects with FASD may struggle to read. In addition to this, suspects with FASD may be easily distracted and as such may not have the mental capacity to pay attention when their rights are being explained (McLachlan, 2021).

The cognitive and social impairments of a suspect with FASD will impact their ability to participate in an interview. Suspects with FASD have been found to be highly suggestible, impulsive, overly trusting of others including strangers, display mental immaturity, and have a high drive to please authority figures (Brown et al., 2020). These characteristics may lead to false confessions as suspects with FASD might impulsively waive their rights, go along with suggestions during interviews, and change their story multiple times. The latter can be especially damaging for a suspect with FASD as changing statements is often perceived as an indication of lying (Brown et al., 2020). Further, credulity—the tendency for a person to accept information as correct and true, even though it is unbelievable and there is no actual evidence—and gullibility—the ease with which a person can be manipulated or tricked—are two psychosocial vulnerabilities present in suspects with FASD (Brown et al., 2020). These two vulnerabilities are related to interrogative suggestibility (see Chapter 8 for further discussion of suggestibility with respect to children as suspects).

Gudjonsson and Clark (1986) identified three main components of interrogative suggestibility, namely: uncertainty as to the "correct" answers to the interviewer's questions (including the perception that there is a "correct" answer to the interviewer's question);

interpersonal trust in the authority of the interviewer—that could include multiple types of interviews (e.g., police, mental health clinician, doctor, social worker); and a reluctance to admit to not knowing answers to the interviewer's questions (Gudjonsson and Clark, 1986 as cited by Brown et al., 2020, p. 3). Unsurprisingly, people with FASD score high on interrogative suggestibility, and as such will likely display the three components when being interviewed by police. This will affect the quality of their interview, and increase the possibility of false confessions. In sum, there are various social and psychological impairments associated with FASD, with all of them having a distinct impact on the integrity of the interview. As such special care needs to be taken when interviewing a suspect with FASD.

Implications for interviewing a suspect with ASD

There are various symptoms of ASD which can severely impact a suspect's experience and participation in an interview (Chown, 2010). These specific symptoms, such as dislike of new situations, severe communication difficulties, and resistance to change, are often inherently linked with police interviews and mean that interviews can be extremely stressful, and even traumatic, for a suspect with ASD. In particular, changes in routine can be extremely difficult for a suspect with ASD (Chown, 2010). Depending on the severity of the disorder, cognitive limitations may result in the suspect having difficulty understanding what is happening, and can include understanding their rights. Suspects with ASD can be at risk of self-incrimination because even when they do not understand the caution, they might indicate they do in order to please the interviewer (Hepworth, 2017). Symbol-based information sheets explaining the caution have been trialled with people who have ASD, and there are indications they may be a good alternative to written or spoken explanations (Hepworth, 2017).

Some interviewing techniques such as the Cognitive Interview might be problematic when interviewing a suspect with ASD (Maras et al., 2018). Studies have found that changes need to be made not only to the communication style, but also to questions asked. Very open-ended questions can be counterproductive for suspects with ASD and more direct, concrete questions need to be used to reduce ambiguity (Maras et al., 2018). Other simple changes, such as modifying the layout of the interview room, changing locations, or not sitting in the suspect's personal space, have been shown to be effective in assisting with sensory or emotional needs of the suspect (Maras et al., 2018).

Guidelines for interviewing a suspect with FASD

Given all these challenges it might seem impossible to conduct a fair interview with a suspect who has FASD. However, Brown and colleagues (2022b, p. 3) after reviewing the extended literature provided various tips for interviewing people with FASD which can assist in reducing suggestibility:

1. Use simple and concrete language.
2. Avoid leading, double-barrelled, or repetitive questions.
3. Do not introduce misleading or inaccurate information.
4. Allow adequate time to process, understand, and consider information.
5. Verify that the individual comprehends any important information.
6. Respect the individual's personal space, including avoiding close contact.
7. Do not use direct or implied threats such as supposed implications for child custody, access to benefits, or any other pressures commonly utilised in legal proceedings.
8. Select an environment that minimises distractions, such as noise or interruptions.

9. Avoid fatiguing the individual—keep interactions short and offer regular breaks.
10. Always try to corroborate any self-reported information with other sources like official records, other witnesses, and family members due to high suggestibility or confabulation (Brown et al., 2022b, p. 3).

Guidelines for interviewing a suspect with ASD

Hepworth and colleagues (2017) suggest the following for use of the PEACE model with suspects who have ASD:

- *Engage and explain.* Social interactions can be stressful for people with ASD. They can struggle to establish empathy, and small talk can induce anxiety. As such, rapport building can be difficult, and may be counterproductive. Moreover, given that suspects with ASD may be more compliant than suspects without ASD, it is important to make sure they understand the process when explaining it, and not just agree as a desire to please the interviewer. To assess understanding, a suspect with ASD could be asked to repeat the caution back in their own words.
- *Account.* Using open-ended questions (such as in the Cognitive Interview) can increase inaccuracies in reporting by suspects with ASD as they may struggle with things such as providing a temporal order of experience, remembering experiences in context, and determining what information is important to report without incriminating themselves. An AA is needed at this point of the interview. It is preferred this is not a person familiar to the suspect, as it can impact the misinterpretation if information (i.e., if the AA is a close family member or friend of the suspect who is familiar with their communication style—they may not realise that the interviewer is misinterpreting statements, Hepworth et al., 2017, p. 217).
- *Clarification.* The use of leading questions is always discouraged but should particularly be avoided when questioning a suspect with ASD. Suspects with ASD are exceptionally suggestible and leading or forced choice questions may result in a suspect with ASD choosing an answer they think is implied in either the question or by the interviewer. It is strongly suggested that a communication and language expert make an assessment before the interview and sits in the interview to actively support the suspect.
- *Closure.* This phase should be used to explain what will happen next, and as such can reduce anxiety in a suspect with ASD. The presence of an AA is needed to make sure the suspect understands the summary presented and what they agree to when closing the interview, so as to not incriminate themselves at this last stage.

Conclusion

Intellectual disorders as well as Foetal Alcohol Spectrum Disorder and Autism Spectrum Disorder are all overrepresented in suspects in the criminal justice system. Moreover, the impairments caused by the respective disorders have a profound effect on the vulnerabilities during investigative interviews. Comprehension of waiving their rights, suggestibility, compliance, and understanding questions are all impacted by these disabilities and as such should be accommodated for during interviews. Various adjustments to standard (Cognitive) interview procedures are provided for each impairment. Some of these might be counterintuitive, such as moving away from very open-ended questions for those with ASD; however, these are necessary for specific conditions. Integrity of the interview can be improved by identification of and adjustment for each condition, and can assist in ensuring, to the extent possible, the admissibility of evidence gathered during the interview.

References

Allely, C.S., & Mukherjee, R. (2019). Suggestibility, false confessions and competency to stand trial in individuals with fetal alcohol spectrum disorders: Current concerns and recommendations. *Journal of Criminal Psychology, 9*(4), 166–172

Bradley, K. J. C. B. (2009). *The Bradley Report: Lord Bradley's review of people with mental health problems or learning disabilities in the criminal justice system* (Vol. 7). London: Department of Health.

Bronson, J., Maruschak, L.M., & Berzofsky, M. (2015). *Disabilities among prison and jail inmates, 2011–12.* US Department of Justice Bureau of Justice Statistics.

Brown, J., Asp, E., Carter, M.N., Spiller, V., & Bishop-Deaton, D. (2020). Suggestibility and confabulation among individuals with fetal alcohol spectrum disorder: A review for criminal justice, forensic mental health, and legal interviewers. *International Journal of Law and Psychiatry, 73*, 101646.

Brown, J., Madore, E., Carter, M.N., Spiller, V., & Jozan, A. (2022b). Fetal alcohol spectrum disorder (FASD) and suggestibility: A survey of United States federal case law. *International Journal of Law and Psychiatry, 80*, 101763.

Chown, N. (2010). 'Do you have any difficulties that I may not be aware of?' A study of autism awareness and understanding in the UK police service. *International Journal of Police Science & Management, 12*(2), 256–273.

Christiansen, A., Minich, N.M., & Clark, M. (2021). Pilot survey: Police understanding of autism spectrum disorder. *Journal of Autism and Developmental Disorders*, 1–8.

Cunial, K.J., & Kebbell, M.R. (2017). Police perceptions of ADHD in youth interviewees. *Psychology, Crime & Law, 23*(5), 509–526.

Dowse, L., Rowe, S., Baldry, E., & Baker, M. (2021). *Police responses to people with disability*. Sydney: University of New South Wales.

Freckelton, I. (2011). Autism spectrum disorders and the criminal law. *A comprehensive book on autism spectrum disorders* (pp. 249–272). Published by InTech

Gudjonsson, G.H., & Clark, N.K. (1986). Suggestibility in police interrogation: A social, psychological model. *Social Behaviour, 1*, 83–104.

Gudjonsson, G.H., Sigurdsson, J.F., Bragason, O.O., Newton, A.K., & Einarsson, E. (2008). Interrogative suggestibility, compliance and false confessions among prisoners and their relationship with attention deficit hyperactivity disorder (ADHD) symptoms. *Psychological Medicine, 38*(7), 1037–1044.

Henshaw, M., Spivak, B., & Thomas, S.D. (2018). Striking the right balance: Police experience, perceptions and use of independent support persons during interviews involving people with intellectual disability. *Journal of Applied Research in Intellectual Disabilities, 31*(2), e201–e211.

Hepworth, D. (2017). A critical review of current police training and policy for autism spectrum disorder. *Journal of Intellectual Disabilities and Offending Behaviour, 8*, 212–222.

Holloway, C.A., Munro, N., Jackson, J., Phillips, S., & Ropar, D. (2020). Exploring the autistic and police perspectives of the custody process through a participative walkthrough. *Research in Developmental Disabilities, 97*, 103545.

Maras, K.L., Mulcahy, S., Crane, L.M., Hawken, T., & Memon, A. (2018). Obtaining best evidence from the autistic interviewee: Police-reported challenges, legal requirements and psychological research-based recommendations. *Investigative Interviewing: Research and Practice, 9*(1), 52–60.

McLachlan, K. (2021). Evaluating competency in defendants with fetal alcohol spectrum disorder. In *Evaluating fetal alcohol spectrum disorders in the forensic context* (pp. 397–425). Springer.

Mogavero, M.C. (2020). An exploratory examination of intellectual disability and mental illness associated with alleged false confessions. *Behavioral Sciences & the Law, 38*(4), 299–316.

Murphy, G., & Clare, I.C. (1998). People with learning disabilities as offenders or alleged offenders in the UK criminal justice system. *Journal of the Royal Society of Medicine, 91*(4), 178–182.

Schatz, S.J. (2018). Interrogated with intellectual disabilities: The risks of false confession. *Stanford Law Review, 70*, 643.

Young, S., Goodwin, E.J., Sedgwick, O., & Gudjonsson, G.H. (2013). The effectiveness of police custody assessments in identifying suspects with intellectual disabilities and attention deficit hyperactivity disorder. *BMC Medicine, 11*(1), 1–11.

Chapter 11

Culturally and Linguistically Diverse (CaLD) and First Nations suspects

Celine van Golde, Jane Tudor-Owen and David Gee

Executive summary

Cultural and Linguistic diversity can provide challenges during interviews. These challenges reflect the vulnerabilities of CaLD suspects. While often named under the same moniker, First Nations suspects are different to CaLD suspects as their vulnerabilities need distinct approaches due to their historical position within their countries of origin. Given the importance of comprehension and production of language for interviews, both CaLD and First Nations suspects should be provided with an interpreter if needed. Moreover, their cultural background should be taken into consideration when evaluating their attitudes and behaviours during the interview. Lastly, these cultural influences should also be recognised when assessing the information provided.

Adjustments should be made to the interview process to accommodate cultural and religious customs and rules. Questions should be carefully worded and constructed, and comprehensions should be checked regularly throughout the interview. In the case of First Nations suspects a support person should be present. If these accommodations are made for CaLD and First Nations suspects, the integrity and fairness of their interviews is protected as much as possible. This chapter will provide an overview of the CaLD and First Nations suspects, their perspectives on police, the use of interpreters, cultural influences on interviews for both CaLD and First Nations suspects, and interview guidelines.

Introduction

Culturally and Linguistically Diverse (CaLD) suspects are classified in research as those who do not live in their country of birth; speak a different language at home than that spoken in their country of residence; or have impaired proficiency in the language spoken in the country of residence (Pham et al., 2021). However, a person does not need to meet all these three criteria to be considered a CaLD suspect. Pham and colleagues further indicated that indigenous suspects (such as Aboriginal and Torres Strait Islander peoples in Australia and First Nations peoples in Canada), who are often considered part of the CaLD suspect group, should actually be considered separately: "Indigenous people are the original inhabitants of the land and contribute an important part of the cultural and linguistic diversity of the country" (Pham et al., 2021 p. 1). As such, this chapter will discuss research and guidelines on interviewing these two groups separately; however, the reader should keep in mind that, while distinct, various findings discussed will be applicable to both CaLD and First Nations suspects.

Increased global mobility (notwithstanding the recent COVID-19 pandemic) has resulted in an increase in CaLD populations around the world. For example, Maddux (2010) found a steady increase in CaLD peoples living in the United States (US) during the 1980s and 1990s.

DOI: 10.4324/9781003145998-14

This accumulated to 47 million people who spoke English as a second language (ESL) in the United States in 2003. Similar trends are seen in other countries, with Ireland having a CaLD population of 15% (Conway et al., 2022); Australia reporting about 25% ESL people living in the state of New South Wales (Howes, 2020); and Sweden even having over half of their population speaking a non-native language at home (Maddux, 2010). However, this global migration presents challenges. For example, Conway and colleagues (2022) reported that migrants in Ireland were more at risk of ending up in the criminal justice system, with 23% of prisoners indicating that they were not Irish nationals. Moreover, each CaLD person brings with them their own (cultural) beliefs, attitudes, and behaviours towards the criminal justice system (Schermuly & Forbes, 2019). Importantly, interviewers should not operate on the basis of unchecked assumptions.

First Nations Australians and Canadians

There is a vast variety in cultural and socio-economic backgrounds amongst Aboriginal and Torres Strait Islander peoples in Australia. This is represented in the many different languages and cultural practices around Australia (Beckett & Graham, 2015). While not all Aboriginal and Torres Strait Islander peoples may be vulnerable there is a glaring overrepresentation of Aboriginal and Torres Strait Islander peoples in the legal system (both as victims and suspects), in mental and physical health statistics, and within the lower socio-economic community (Beckett & Graham, 2015). As such, it becomes clear that when an Aboriginal or Torres Strait Islander person becomes a suspect within a criminal investigation there is the possibility of a multitude of vulnerabilities that need to be considered. That this consideration does not always happen is reflected by Roach (2015). Their findings showed that compared to the underrepresentation of First Nations peoples in Canada and Australia in the general population, there is an overrepresentation not only in prison populations but also amongst the wrongfully convicted (see also Stratton & Sigamoney, 2020). Roach (2015) found that it was especially First Nations women who were at risk of wrongful convictions as they were more likely to plead guilty.

Roach's findings indicate some of the challenges First Nations peoples face within the criminal justice system. First of all, Nakane (2007) showed the vulnerability of First Nations peoples with regard to understanding the caution. Specifically, they provided a case example to demonstrate that First Nations peoples, while answering "yes" to comprehension check questions about the caution, might not understand the meaning of the caution. Rather, answering "yes" to the comprehension questions might be indicative of compliance with authority or cultural demand characteristics. Indeed, research shows that amongst Aboriginal and Torres Strait Islander societies in Australia, "if a white person asks you many questions, especially in a pressured situation, the best thing is to say 'yes'" (Beckett & Graham, 2015, p. 6).

In this chapter, perceptions of CaLD and First Nations peoples of police will be discussed, and the use of interpreters during interviews with CaLD and First Nations peoples. These sections will be followed by considerations when interviewing CaLD and First Nations peoples, and recommendations to standard interview practices.

The relationship between CaLD peoples and police

How fair interactions between community members and police are considered to be is called Procedural Justice (Cole et al., 2020). Procedural Justice is closely related to perceptions of legitimacy of the police, which in turn predict compliance and cooperation from community members with the police (Schermuly & Forbes, 2019). Throughout history, a global trend emerges where CaLD, Indigenous, and lower socio-economic status (SES) people often have fraud relationships with police (Cole et al., 2020; Schermuly & Forbes, 2019). These fraud relationships cause distrust both in CaLD peoples and police, which can cause over-policing of CaLD groups and in turn even more distrust on both sides. As such, a vicious circle continues where this initial distrust hampers cooperation, communication, and assistance between the two parties (Cole et al., 2020). One potential explanation for the initial poor relationship between police and CaLD peoples is the fact that migrants' opinions about the justice system are often based on (experiences with) police in their native country (Schermuly & Forbes, 2019; Stephen & Perpetual, 2013). While not necessarily representative of the police in their current country of residence, the snowball effect of having these opinions can increase the likelihood that CaLD peoples actually end up having interactions with police. Moreover, these opinions will then further influence CaLD peoples' participation in police interviews.

The relationship between First Nations peoples and police

There is a historically complicated relationship between First Nations peoples and police, resulting in continuing hostility and/or distrust in the present day for some (Beckett & Graham, 2015; Cao, 2014). The origins of this fraught relationship are the colonisation of both Australia and Canada, when First Nations peoples were forcefully removed from their land, put in reserves or missions, had their children removed and forcefully adopted out, and their language and expressions controlled; each of which was overseen and enforced by police (Cao, 2014; O'Brien, 2021). Not only did these practices instil an ongoing distrust of police in First Nations peoples, they further shaped their socio-economic positions today (which increases their vulnerability; O'Brien, 2021). At the same time, today First Nations peoples are overpoliced. O'Brien (2021) reported that young Maori people in New Zealand were in contact with the police almost three times as often as their non-Maori counterparts, and First Nations Australian men were reported constantly being stopped, searched, and questioned by police. Similarly, First Nations Canadians were two-and-a-half times more likely to come into contact with police involuntarily than non-First Nations Canadians, with voluntariness of contact being a determining predictor of having confidence in police (Alberton et al., 2019). The continuing effect of the historical trauma inflicted on First Nations peoples is an extensive topic in itself. For the purpose of this chapter, it is important to keep in mind that perceptions held by First Nations peoples towards police will affect their attitude to and participation in interviews.

Interpreters

There are a substantial number of CaLD peoples living in countries around the world (Lee & Hu, 2021). These CaLD peoples are more likely to come into contact with the police (Conway et al., 2022), and are vulnerable as they do not necessarily speak or understand the language well. Consequently, interpreting has become an essential part of policing (Goodman-Delahunty & Martschuk, 2016; Hale, 2019). This is reflected in the fact that access to an interpreter is considered an essential right for a fair trial in the United Nations International Covenant on Civil and Political Rights (ICCPR) and the Council of Europe's European Convention on Human Rights (ECHR) (Conway et al., 2022). This right extends beyond the trial to police interviews as well. However, while acknowledging this right, neither the ICCPR nor the ECHR have actually provided guidelines on who can be an interpreter or what training they should do. Moreover, there is actually no system for quality assurance for interpreters, nor is it compulsory for legal interpreters to be adequately trained and qualified (Hale, 2019; Lee & Hu, 2021).

As discussed in Chapter 3, conducting an interview with an interpreter present is both time consuming and complex. The three-way communication results in extended interview times and police officers have mentioned various difficulties brought on by having a third person in the interview (Howes, 2020). Some of these difficulties include the effects of the interpreting process on the ability to build and maintain rapport, and making sure that the interpreter's behaviours do not impact the neutrality of the interview or the experience of the suspect (Howes, 2019). Moreover, Hu and Naka (2022) found that it was quite common for interpreters to omit certain details (such as times and places) especially when translating longer utterances. This omission of details by interpreters would lead to a suspect appearing to be providing less (detailed) information (Hu & Naka, 2020).

Nonetheless, interpreters are essential in interviews with CaLD suspects who are unable to adequately communicate with police officers in an interview. The main reason being that they help facilitate fairness and participation to a suspect who would otherwise be unable to participate, or understand the legal system (Howes, 2019). In Chapter 1 we outlined that being interviewed in and of itself engenders vulnerability in a suspect. Being unable to understand or communicate further increases this vulnerability. Moreover, the legal language used in police interviews can be quite complex, and not understanding what is said or asked can carry serious consequences (Conway et al., 2022). While some CaLD suspects might be able to communicate appropriately in everyday situations, this does not imply that they have the ability to do the same in an interview context (Conway et al., 2022). This is particularly the case with regard to understanding the caution and suspect's right and decisions around waiving these.

Nakane (2007) investigated the efficacy of interpreters' communication of suspect rights (i.e., caution), by reviewing interviews between Japanese-speaking suspects and English-speaking police officers. One of the issues identified by Nakane was interpreters' own understanding of the caution. Legal language is complicated and can be difficult to understand even for a trained interpreter. This was shown in Nakane's findings where interpreters shifted between verbatim translation and meaning-based translation, reflecting where the interpreter struggled with understanding the caution themselves. This lack of understanding of legal concepts has bigger implications, as the quality of the translation will influence the understanding by the suspect. Misunderstanding by the suspect can result in self-incriminating behaviour and false confessions. Moreover, both police and the non-English-speaking suspect may be oblivious to ignorance of interpreters and as such unduly accept false information.

Implications for interviews with people who are CaLD

There are various cultural determinants which can impact CaLD suspects' behaviours and communications during an interview, increasing their vulnerability (some of these might be applicable to First Nations peoples as well). First of all, the cultural orientation a person comes from can influence their participation in an interview (Hope & Gabbert, 2019). Individualistic cultures revolve around an individual, compared to collectivist cultures where the focus is on society as a whole, "the greater good" (Anakwah et al., 2020a). This focus on the group rather than the individual can impact how CaLD suspects answer questions and can even influence the risk of false confessions. CaLD suspects from collectivist culture in this situation will be influenced by culturally determined reporting norms (Anakwah et al., 2020a). Another example of a characteristic of collectivist cultures is the endorsement of hierarchy in social situations. This respect for authority may inhibit spontaneous communication with authority figures (such as police officers), and reduces the number of details shared (Anakwah et al., 2020a; 2020b). This self-censoring, or inhibition, by a CaLD suspect during an interview can negatively impact the perceptions of the suspect (e.g., they can come across as lying or insincere).

An additional difference in reporting norms between collectivist and individualistic cultures can be explained by parent–child interactions (Anakwah et al., 2020a; 2020b). That is, within individualistic cultures parent–child communication focuses on elaboration and feedback. As such, children in these cultures learn the importance of providing details and elaboration. This is in contrast with collectivist cultures where the emphasis is on self-restraint, which limits information sharing (Anakwah et al., 2020b). These cultural differences can directly influence response styles in forensic interviews. However, the adaptability of humankind needs to be taken into consideration as well. Specifically, when people move to a new country they will adapt to the new culture. At the same time, they will retain (some) of the norms of their own culture (this is called acculturation; Anakwah et al., 2020b). The degree of acculturation will determine how CaLD suspects' responses in an interview should be interpreted. As Anakwah et al. (2020b) state:

> thus, while it is important that forensic interviews consider the cultural background of the interviewee, taking cultural background into account when interviewing eyewitnesses who are migrants, without an appreciation of whether acculturation factors might influence their memory reports, may be counterproductive.
>
> (p. 240)

Implications for interviews with First Nations peoples

The whole concept of an investigative interview is at odds with Aboriginal and Torres Strait Islander culture. Beckett and Graham (2015) stated that direct questions are not used by many Aboriginal and Torres Strait Islander peoples when they want to find out personal, or significant, details. Instead, they may share some personal information relating the same information they want to find out about. As such, seeking information is a two-way exchange, unlike standard investigative interviews, which are relying on direct questioning. Another example which emphasises the disconnect between Aboriginal and Torres Strait Islander culture and forensic interviewing is the use of silence in conversations. Aboriginal peoples are happy to sit in silence and wait till the other person is ready to provide information; silence is part of the information-seeking process. This is in contrast with Western societies which see silence as a breakdown in communication (Beckett & Graham, 2015).

Interviewing guidelines

It is not only the fact that a suspect is non-English speaking that may render them particularly vulnerable. It may be that people in their culture have a historically complicated relationship with police, resulting in hostility and/or distrust (Beckett & Graham, 2015). It is also important to consider how the suspect may come across to a judge and/or jury in the event the interview is played in court, and to what extent any negative impact may be mitigated (Beckett & Graham, 2015).

Khawaja (2011) provided some tips when interviewing CaLD clients as a forensic psychologist. While interviewing a suspect of a crime naturally has a completely different objective, there are some similarities which could be applied within a CaLD suspect's interview.

- Be prepared for interviews to take longer. Even if the suspect is able to participate in an interview without an interpreter, cultural differences might mean that the interview will take longer anyway.
- Seek information about the suspect's cultural background. Their cultural rules, or religion, can influence who they can talk to, and how they respond to questions. However, keep in mind the concept of acculturation, and the influence this might have on alignment of the suspect with their culture.
- In many non-Western cultures it is important to match the gender between suspect and interviewer. Make sure to further adjust interview behaviours such as eye contact and distance between the suspect and you to accommodate cultural nuances.
- Investigate the reason the CaLD suspect migrated. Research shows an influence of migration motivation on vulnerability, such that those who were forced or unwilling to migrate have increased vulnerability during an interview. Moreover, it is useful to know if the suspect has a support network or is geographically isolated.

When it comes to interviews with Aboriginal and Torres Strait Islander peoples, Martine Powell (2000) proposed the use of the acronym, PRIDE, to highlight key aspects to consider: P is Prior knowledge about the interviewee and the wider context; R is Rapport with the interviewee; I is Interpretive assistance if required; D is Diverse array of hypotheses (keeping an open mind and avoiding confirmation basis); and E is Effective techniques for obtaining a free narrative (remembering that this may look different than in an interview with someone from a different culture).

In *R v Anunga* (1976) 11 ALR 412, 414-415 Forster J set out guidelines for interviewing Aboriginal and Torres Strait Islander suspects. While these rules were first articulated as guidelines to be followed for police interactions with Aboriginal and Torres Strait Islander peoples in the Northern Territory, they have since been incorporated in guidelines for interviewing in other Australian jurisdictions including, for example, Western Australia (Corruption and Crime Commission, 2018). The *Anunga* guidelines are as follows:

1. An interpreter should be utilised where the suspect is not able to understand or communicate in English.
2. A "prisoner's friend" or support person should be present.
3. Be careful when administering the caution and ask the suspect to explain the caution in their own words to check their understanding.
4. Ask non-leading questions and be mindful of tone and manner to avoid indicating a preferred response.
5. Confessions must be corroborated.
6. Provide fluids, food, and the opportunity for comfort breaks.
7. Do not interview a suspect who is "disabled by illness or drunkenness or tiredness" (p. 415) or question a suspect for an unreasonable length of time.
8. Assist in securing legal advice and/or stop the interview when requested.
9. If clothing is removed for a forensic procedure, ensure replacement clothing is provided.

Additionally, in their guide for lawyers, Beckett and Graham (2015) provided general guidelines for taking instructions from Aboriginal or Torres Strait Islander clients that can also be applied in the interviewing context:

- Avoid negative questions ("You weren't there, were you?").
- Define unfamiliar or "legal" words.
- Avoid compound (multiple) questions.
- Signpost when you are changing the topic.
- Be careful (or avoid) talking about hypothetical situations.
- It may be an indication the suspect has not understood the question if their response mirrors the interviewer's language too closely.
- "Yes" may not mean "yes", it may be the suspect trying to please the interviewer or speed up the process.
- Silence or saying "I don't know" may be a way of the suspect communicating they are not comfortable disclosing the information in front of the people present (e.g., interpreter or support person). Try asking in a different way before taking the silence as an indication the suspect is unwilling to answer the question.

Case study

Our cultures and customs influence how we interact with each other. When two different cultures meet in non-investigative situations this can lead to a clash, or to an appreciation (and sometimes celebration) of those different from us. Adaptations of customs can happen when acculturation takes place. In general, awareness and understanding of our cultural differences will facilitate successful interactions. This is especially the case when it comes to investigative interviewing, where misunderstanding of cultural rules, customs, and etiquettes can have detrimental effects on the access to justice for those from other cultures.

Beckett and Graham (2015) demonstrated this in a confronting manner when tabulating work conducted by Eades in 2003. Specifically, they showed how behaviours and customs by Aboriginal and Torres Strait Islander peoples were in direct contrast to those used in Western legal institutions and, as a result, put them at a direct risk of having their access to justice denied.

For example, silence when being asked a question is interpreted in Western society as unwillingness to cooperate or ignorance. However, for a person who identifies as Aboriginal or Torres Strait Islander, staying silent may be a sign of thoughtfulness, and recognition of the value of time. Similarly, for some people who identify as Aboriginal or Torres Strait Islander, it is a sign of disrespect when you look an older person and/or someone you should respect in the eye. Avoidance of gaze, in Western legal settings, is an indicator of lying. When Western legal professionals want to find out a lot of information, they will ask a lot of questions. For a person who identifies as Aboriginal or Torres Strait Islander, asking a lot of questions is considered very rude and ultimately ineffective if you want to find out any information. Relatedly, many Aboriginal and Torres Strait Islander peoples will not interrupt you with questions when you are telling a story. Interruptions make it more difficult to be accurate and consistent. However, legal professionals in Western society rely on asking questions to receive specific information (Beckett & Graham, 2015, p. 6). While these examples are just a fraction of the cultural differences experienced between Western legal institutions and Aboriginal and Torres Strait Islander peoples, they convey how easily cultural misunderstandings can have severe consequences in legal settings such as interviews with suspects.

Conclusion

Interviewing CaLD suspects can be a complicated task given the many considerations that need to be given to their cultural and linguistic vulnerabilities. Similar considerations need to be given when interviewing First Nations peoples. For both groups, the linguistic diversity can cause issues with understanding not only legal language, but even common questions asked. In these cases, it is the right of the suspect to have an interpreter present, which will facilitate the fairness of the interviews as well as the integrity of the information gathered through the interview. Cultural differences should be acknowledged as well, as they can strongly influence the attitude to, and participation in, the interview.

Assessing if a suspect comes from a collectivist or individualistic culture, as well as their previous experience with law enforcement, will be detrimental to the effectiveness of interviews with CaLD suspects. Similarly, when it comes to First Nations suspects, besides their cultural attitudes to information gathering, transgenerational trauma should be acknowledged as it can influence distrust in police. It is important to keep in mind that these vulnerabilities can be accommodated for. When incorporating the above-outlined suggestions for interviewing CaLD and First Nations suspects during interviews, integrity and fairness can be achieved.

References

Alberton, A.M., Gorey, K.M., Angell, G.B., & McCue, H.A. (2019). Intersection of Indigenous peoples and police: Questions about contact and confidence. *Canadian Journal of Criminology and Criminal Justice*, *61*(4), 101–119.

Anakwah, N., Horselenberg, R., Hope, L., Amankwah-Poku, M., & Van Koppen, P.J. (2020a). Cross-cultural differences in eyewitness memory reports. *Applied Cognitive Psychology*, *34*(2), 504–515.

Anakwah, N., Horselenberg, R., Hope, L., Amankwah-Poku, M., & van Koppen, P.J. (2020b). The acculturation effect and eyewitness memory reports among migrants. *Legal and Criminological Psychology*, *25*(2), 237–256.

Beckett, S., & Graham, F. (2015). Asking aboriginal people questions. A paper about calling evidence from Aboriginal clients and witnesses and the application of the Evidence Act 1995 (NSW). Presented at the 2015 Conference of the Environment and Planning Law Association, 16 October 2015, Sydney, NSW, Australia

Cao, L. (2014). Aboriginal people and confidence in the police. *Canadian Journal of Criminology and Criminal Justice*, *56*(5), 499–526.

Cole, L.M., April, K., & Trinkner, R.J. (2020). The black and white reality: Historical and post-Ferguson era perspectives on public attitudes toward the police. In *Advances in psychology and law* (pp. 267–299). Springer, Cham.

Conway, V., Daly, Y., & McEvoy, G. (2022). Interpretation in Police Stations: Lawyers' Perspectives on Rights and Realities. *Journal of Human Rights Practice*, *13*(3), 606–628.

Corruption and Crime Commission. (2018). *The implementation of recommendations arising from the commission's investigation into operation aviemore: A further report*. Government of Western Australia.

Goodman-Delahunty, J., & Martschuk, N. (2016). Risks and benefits of interpreter-mediated police interviews. *Varstvoslovje: Journal of Criminal Justice & Security*, *18*(4), 451–471.

Hale, S., Goodman-Delahunty, J., & Martschuk, N. (2019). Interpreter performance in police interviews. Differences between trained interpreters and untrained bilinguals. *The Interpreter and Translator Trainer*, *13*(2), 107–131.

Hope, L., & Gabbert, F. (2019). Interviewing witnesses and victims. In N. Brewer & A. B. Douglass (Eds.), Psychological science and the law (pp. 56–74). New York: The Guildford Press.

Howes, L.M. (2019). Community interpreters' experiences of police investigative interviews: How might interpreters' insights contribute to enhanced procedural justice?. *Policing and Society*, *29*(8), 887–905.

Howes, L.M. (2020). Interpreted investigative interviews under the PEACE interview model: Police interviewers' perceptions of challenges and suggested solutions. *Police Practice and Research*, *21*(4), 333–350.

Hu, Z., & Naka, M. (2020). Using temporary interpreters in mock forensic interviews. *Journal of Police and Criminal Psychology*, 1–9.

Hu, Z., & Naka, M. (2022). Eyewitness testimony in native and second languages. *Psychology, Crime & Law*, 1–17.

Khawaja, N. (2011). Effective interviewing of culturally and linguistically diverse clients. *In-Psych: The Bulletin of the Australian Psychological Society*, *33*(3), 1–1.

Lee, J., & Huh, J. (2021). A need for building an ethical and trusting partnership between police officers and interpreters: Findings from South Korea. *Translation & Interpreting*, *13*(2), 29–44.

Maddux, J. (2010). Recommendations for forensic evaluators conducting interpreter-mediated interviews. *International Journal of Forensic Mental Health*, *9*(1), 55–62.

Nakane, I. (2007). Problems in communicating the suspect's rights in interpreted police interviews. *Applied Linguistics*, *28*(1), 87–112.

O'Brien, G. (2021). Racial profiling, surveillance and over-policing: The over-incarceration of young first nations males in Australia. *Social Sciences*, *10*(2), 68.

Pham, T.T.L., Berecki-Gisolf, J., Clapperton, A., O'Brien, K.S., Liu, S., & Gibson, K. (2021). Definitions of culturally and linguistically diverse (CALD): A literature review of epidemiological research in Australia. *International Journal of Environmental Research and Public Health*, *18*(2), 737.

Powell, M. (2000). PRIDE: The essential elements of a forensic interview with an Aboriginal person. *Australian Psychologist*, *35*, 186–192. doi: 10.1080/00050060008257477

Roach, K. (2015). The wrongful conviction of Indigenous people in Australia and Canada. *Flinders Law Journal*, *17*, 203.

Schermuly, A.C., & Forbes-Mewett, H. (2019). Police legitimacy: Perspectives of migrants and non-migrants in Australia. *Journal of Criminological Research, Policy and Practice*, *5*(1), 50–63.

Stephen, E., & Perpetual, C. (2013). Migrants' perception of the police: Should it be a cause for concern in Finland?. *European Journal of Criminology*, *10*(5), 555–571.

Stratton, G., & Sigamoney, A. (2020). Why we don't see race: How Australia has overlooked race as an influence on miscarriages of justice. *Race and Justice*, 1–16 2153368720922294.

Chapter 12

Interviewing in the context of gender and sexual diversity

Jane Tudor-Owen, Celine van Golde and David Gee

Executive summary

As with all of the specific vulnerabilities addressed in Part II of this book, not everyone who identifies as gender- and/or sexually-diverse will consider themselves to be vulnerable on that basis. It may also be that police would not have initially considered this to be a vulnerability. However, when we consider the importance of rapport in interviews, it is not hard to realise why it is important to recognise and respect gender and sexual diversity in the interview context.

This chapter is focused on providing some context and rationale to explain why a person's gender and sexuality is important to consider in policing and in interviewing specifically. As previously noted at length in Chapter 1, the experience of being interviewed as a suspect engenders a level of vulnerability and for suspects who further identify as gender- and/or sexually-diverse, this vulnerability may well be heightened. In part, this may be due to the historically complicated relationship between police and gender- and sexually-diverse people. In some countries, the increase in gender and sexual diversity amongst police officers is an indication this relationship may be improving. The chapter also provides practical suggestions to reduce assumptions about gender and sexuality, thereby encouraging inclusive policing practices in interviewing.

Introduction

As discussed in Chapter 1, vulnerability takes many forms and it is important to acknowledge at the outset that there are individuals who may identify as gender- and/or sexually-diverse who may not consider themselves to be vulnerable as a result. Although understanding of gender and sexual diversity is growing, it is still useful to examine language used to describe the way in which people might identify in relation to their gender and sexuality.

The acronym LGBTQIA+ is used commonly to refer broadly to gender and sexual diversity, as it encompasses a wide population: Lesbian, Gay, Bisexual, Transsexual, Questioning, Intersex, and Asexual. The + symbol included as part of the acronym recognises that these are just some of the descriptors and there are many who would use alternative terms to describe themselves. It is also necessary to note that these terms refer to identity and do not require any legal or medical responses to validate them. For example, a trans person may or may not have changed their name legally, or be undertaking medical intervention. Regardless, they are transsexual if the gender assigned at birth is not consistent with their identity. There are many resources available online to assist people in understanding what is meant by each of these terms and it is important that professionals such as police officers take the time to educate

DOI: 10.4324/9781003145998-15

themselves. Although it is not always compulsory, increasing numbers of organisations are offering specific training around diversity, including gender and sexual diversity.

The relevance of gender and sexual diversity in a book about safeguarding the interview process for vulnerable suspects may not be immediately clear. The word "cisheteronormative" may be new to some readers but simply put it means that the culture normalises cis (genitals consistent with gender identity) hetero (opposite sex attracted) individuals. It is necessary to first recognise the dominant cisheteronormative culture that is prevalent in many countries across the world, and the implications of living in such a culture for people who do not identify as cisheteronormative. For people who do not identify as cishetero, their experiences growing up in a world where they are consistently "othered" (made to feel different) can take a toll. For example, someone who does not look "female" being questioned each time they enter bathrooms "designated for females" or a male discussing their partner's work, only to have the person assume the partner must be female. Many times, the "othering" is not intentional; however, there are also instances where it is.

It is not enough to say that "times have changed", as there are likely to be deeply rooted responses to long-term system discrimination experienced by members of the LGBTQIA+ community. Depending on the age of the suspect, they might have lived in society in a time where engaging in consensual sexual acts with their partner of the same sex was criminalised. That this was the case, and in many jurisdictions still is, may be enough to position a person in opposition to law enforcement or the criminal justice system more generally, regardless of whether they themselves were the subject of any criminal allegations.

Although great strides have been made with respect to sexual diversity, there is still a way to go. Further, with regard to gender diversity, awareness amongst the general population in most countries is largely in its infancy and advocates are working hard for recognition across all spheres of society, including in the health and legal systems. The struggle for recognition and the fight against discrimination is a current one for gender-diverse members of the community.

When LGBTQIA+ suspects come into contact with interviewers, many will have experienced wide-ranging discrimination from people and society more generally, including police. As such, it is important for interviewers to be aware that there is likely to be an underlying level of vulnerability due to these previous experiences both personally, and more generally. In addition, there are specific aspects of a person's interaction with police as a gender- and/or sexually-diverse person that may be made more difficult. For example, assumptions made regarding gender in assigning an officer to conduct a search. The impact of these prior interactions and current assumptions may then impact the interview, so it is important to firstly minimise this where possible (see below), and then be mindful moving forward.

This chapter will first examine historical attitudes towards the LGBTQIA+ community by police, and vice versa. It will then consider police training, followed by implications for interviewing and a case study to illustrate current trends.

Historical attitudes

Research has shown that some members of the LGBTQIA+ community hold negative perceptions about police. While attitudes appear to be changing in some countries, the historically tense relationship between this community and police may still pose difficulties in current interactions.

Perceptions of LGBTQIA+ victims are more commonly researched than those of LGBTQIA+ suspects. Analysing 1896 incident reports collected between 1990 and 2000 in one state in the United States, Wolff and Cokely (2007) found that perceptions of police conduct improved over this time period; however, negative feedback from the public outnumbered positive feedback with regard to police behaviour. LGBTQIA+ individuals felt victimised by the police who were actually responding to requests for assistance. Over time, the rate of police-initiated contact decreased, as did negative reports of police conduct. Considering implications for interviews with LGBTQIA+ suspects, there would seem to be a high risk that police-initiated contact would be perceived negatively, and potentially more so than by the general population.

Research has also found that some members of the LGBTQA+ community believe that police are more likely to be of assistance with heterosexual members of the community. For example, Finneran and Stephenson (2013) found that while 85% of gay and bisexual males believed police would be helpful or very helpful to a female victim of intimate partner violence, this reduced to 30% with respect to a gay/bisexual male victim. Further, 40% of participants believed police would be unhelpful or very unhelpful for a gay/bisexual male victim in comparison to 4.8% believing this in response to a female victim. In a study examining perceptions of police treatment of minority groups, participants who identified as lesbian, gay, or bisexual were less likely than those identifying as heterosexual to believe that minority groups were treated fairly by police (Owen et al., 2018). There is greater concern regarding police treatment of transgender individuals than lesbian, gay, and bisexual individuals (Owen et al., 2018). This may be due to the relatively recent increase in recognition of transgender individuals in some countries.

Contemporary police culture

Many members of society, including police and thus interviewing officers, have scant knowledge of the associated issues regarding members of society identifying with a sexuality that is viewed as "different" by the remaining populace. This lack can lead to suspicion, intolerance, respect, avoidance, amongst many conflicting behaviours and beliefs, each of which has the potential to add to the vulnerability of a suspect. Their own behavioural responses to their beliefs and value judgements by interviewing officers can actually make the officers themselves feel vulnerable as they may consequently feel uncomfortable operating "out of their own comfort zone". Thus, the situation can be influenced to such an extent that everyone involved in the interview can feel unusually vulnerable.

All the more reason, therefore, for interviewing officers to familiarise themselves with any personal differences from either party that might jeopardise the effectiveness of the interview. The rider to this is that assumptions should not be made by interviewers that all suspects identifying with a particular societal group are thus vulnerable. Due cognisance should be taken from the perspective of the suspect operating within their own norms and values not simply from the perspective of the interviewing officer. Also, not all suspects identified by wider society or indeed "representative" bodies share the same ethos and characteristics as reported. The maxim is to treat the suspect appropriately, not in the same way as others from any community upon which a differential label has been assigned. Suspects should be provided with a service that reflects their individual characteristics rather than through assumed knowledge drawn from whatever source.

It is important that in both the "Preparation and planning" and "Engage and explain" phases of the "PEACE" model that interviewers take the time to establish as thorough a working knowledge as time allows, drawn from empirical sources as well as from the individual suspect, that will mitigate any potential to increase the vulnerability of the suspect in what may already be a vulnerable situation for them. This will include agreeing with the suspect on forms of address so that the suspect is made to feel as comfortable as possible.

Although in some countries society has evolving maturity in embracing diversity regarding lesbian, gay, and bisexual people, this may not be the case for intersex, transgender, binary, and non-binary people. For the gender-diverse population, there may be practical difficulties regarding toilet facilities, "cell allocation", use of pronouns that may all become relevant to the suspect. It is important therefore to ensure that any language used, and assumptions made around sexuality and behaviour are avoided

Police training

Research evaluating LGBTQIA+ training for police officers in the United States found it successful in improving the knowledge and use of LGBTQIA+-affirming strategies in policing (Israel et al., 2014). In this evaluation of a five-hour workshop no changes were noted in interpersonal apprehension pre- and post-training; however, these scores were low which is positive in itself. The finding that knowledge increased following training is important, as the content comprised, amongst other things, information around definitions relevant to the LGBTQIA+ community. Being able to understand a person's identity is the first step to engaging in affirming interactions.

In Australia, some policing agencies employ LGBTQIA+ police liaison officers (Dwyer et al., 2015), but their use is limited at times by the geographical expanse of some states. In particular, this has implications for the rural LGBTQIA+ community (Dwyer et al., 2015). People living in rural areas may be less supportive of the LGBTQIA+ community, perhaps due to less exposure to diversity, and it therefore makes sense there would be concern that police in such areas may also be less supportive, and participants in New South Wales and Queensland identified fearing homophobic responses from police (Dwyer et al., 2015). Research has also indicated that tenure policies in policing agencies have the ability to undermine progress made when effective police liaison officers are relocated to other geographical locations or business units (Dwyer et al., 2015). One police liaison officer interviewed in New South Wales noted that resourcing seems to be "city centric" (Dwyer et al., 2015, p. 235).

Implications for interviews

One main implication for interviewing relates to rapport. Where there exists an historically fragmented relationship, it will be more difficult to build rapport. If LGBTQIA+ individuals fear responses from police when they are in need of assistance, this is even more likely to be the case for suspects. While police participants in LGBTQIA+ training for law enforcement personnel have verbalised that everyone should be treated the same (Israel et al., 2017), it is clear that there are specific aspects of police interactions with gender- and/or sexually-diverse individuals around which police need to be mindful, including interviewing. It is important that training involves both policing agencies and local LGBTQIA+ representatives in order to be effective (Israel et al., 2014).

As with interviewing generally, what occurs before an interview with a gender- or sexually-diverse suspect can have an impact on the interview itself. With the LGBTQIA+ population, particular consideration needs to be given to the conducting of forensic procedures (e.g., body searching). Assumptions about the appropriate gender for the police staff involved need to be checked with the suspect.[1] For transgender suspects, it is important to make enquiries as to their preferred pronouns, being mindful that the individual's outward expression of gender may not correlate with legal documentation provided. Suggestions from law enforcement personnel in Israel and colleagues' (2016) research included asking the person directly for their preferred pronouns, correcting any misgendering, and privately authenticating identifying information. In the context of an interview, this could include differentiating between a legal name and a preferred name, allowing the suspect to indicate which name they would prefer to be used in the interview and being mindful of not assuming gender when a suspect mentions a partner or spouse. For example, if a female suspect discloses their partner can provide an alibi, the follow-up questions should be in gender neutral terms. That is, questioning about what *they* were doing rather than what *he* was doing.

Interview guidelines

Specific resources are available to provide additional guidance with regard to establishing inclusive practices in the workplace. The Law Society in the United Kingdom, for example, has produced guidelines for encouraging inclusive use of pronouns. They suggest the following strategies:[2]

- Use "they/them" until you know someone's pronouns, e.g., "The suspect has been cautioned. I will take them for processing".
- Introduce people carefully using their pronouns so it signals to others what pronouns to use, e.g., "This is Detective Constable Brown, they are attached to X Unit. This is Detective Sergeant Smith, she is attached to Y Unit".
- Listen to how people refer to themselves and adopt what they use.
- Pronouns may have been communicated in correspondence so pay attention for any clues.
- If you are unsure, discreetly ask (e.g., "Sorry, Sam, what are your preferred pronouns?").

Conclusion

Our gender and sexual identity are inherently personal; however, it is not always possible for them to remain private. As such, it is important that these be dealt with sensitively, and that given what we know about the prevalence of gender and sexual diversity, we do not make assumptions; for example, that people are cisgendered and heterosexual by default.

The content of this chapter is designed to provide a brief overview of some of the various circumstances in which gender and sexuality may become important in the course of policing and, more specifically, during an investigative interview. Rather than considering particular interview guidelines, the strategies presented in this chapter encourage police and other practitioners to be aware of assumptions that are typically made, and to endeavour to suspend these. In doing so, it provides the opportunity to practice and promote inclusion and has the potential to impact rapport building positively which in turn has been found to improve the likelihood of a positive interview outcome.

Notes

1 In the absence of agency policy; however, agency policy needs to reflect consideration for the LGBTQIA+ population
2 https://www.lawsociety.org.uk/en/topics/hr-and-people-management/using-pronouns-in-the-workplace

References

Dwyer, A., Ball, M., & Barker, E. (2015). Policing LGBTIQ people in rural spaces: emerging issues and future concerns. *Rural Society, 24*(3), 227–243. doi: 10.1080/10371656.2015.1099264

Finneran, C., & Stephenson, R. (2013). Gay and bisexual men's perceptions of police helpfulness in response to male-male intimate partner violence. *Western Journal of Emergency Medicine, 14*(4), 354–362. doi: 10.5811/westjem.2013.3.15639

Israel, T., Harkness, A., Delucio, K., Ledbetter, J.N., & Avellar, T.R. (2014). Evaluation of police training on LGBTQ issues: Knowledge, interpersonal apprehension, and self-efficacy. *Journal of Police and Criminal Psychology, 29*, 57–67. doi: 10.1007/s11896-013-9132-z

Israel, T., Harkness, A., Avellar, T.R., Delucio, K., Bettergarcia, J.N., & Goodman, J.A. (2016). LGBTQ-affirming policing: Tactics generated by law enforcement personnel. *Journal of Police and Criminal Psychology, 31*, 173–181. doi: 10.1007/s11896-015-9169-2

Israel, T., Bettergarcia, J.N., Delucio, K., Avellar, T.R., Harkness, A., & Goodman, J.A. (2017). Reactions of law enforcement to LGBTQ diversity training. *Human Resource Development Quarterly, 28*(2), 197–226. doi: 10.1002/hrdq.21281

Owen, S.S., Burke, T.W., Few-Demo, A.L., & Natwick, J. (2018). Perceptions of the police by LGBT communities. *American Journal of Criminal Justice, 43*, 668–693. doi: 10.1007/s12103-017-9420-8

Wolff, K.B., & Cokely, C.L. (2007). "To protect and service?": An exploration of police conduct in relation to the gay, lesbian, bisexual, and transgender community. *Sex Cult, 11*, 1–23. doi: 10.1007/s12119-007-9000-z

Chapter 13

Interviewing suspects with a hearing impairment

Celine van Golde, Jane Tudor-Owen and David Gee

Executive summary

Interviewing a d/Deaf suspect can be challenging unless proper considerations are taken. Deaf people are part of a minority community with their own language, history, and customs. As such, they will experience a multitude of vulnerabilities during custodial interview. One obvious vulnerability is communication. In particular, when d/Deaf people rely on sign language, barriers they consequently experience during interviews put them at risk of providing unreliable information or self-incrimination due to no fault of their own.

Interpreters should be engaged if needed, and adjustments should be made to interview practices. Repeated comprehension checks, and evaluation of the information provided by the suspect in light of the fact that sign language has no literal translation to spoken or written language, should be conducted. Acknowledgement of the stress caused by not being able to hear or understand what is happening is essential. Unfamiliar paralanguage such as touching and extended gaze can be expected, and should be interpreted as part of sign language. With these considerations fairness of interviews with d/Deaf suspects can be maximised.

This chapter will provide a definition of d/Deafness, statistics on d/Deafness, an explanation of communication with d/Deaf suspects, the influence on waiving their rights, police experience with d/Deaf suspects, a case study, and considerations for interview guidelines.

Introduction

The World Health Organization (WHO) reported in 2011 that 15% of the world population lives with a disability. Of these 1 billion people, one fifth reported living with severe disabilities (Australian Human Right Committee, 2016). This last number indicates that disabilities can be experienced and affect people in different ways due to the varying extent of the impact. A person *born* with a disability (e.g., cystic fibrosis) will be differently impacted throughout life than a person who becomes quadriplegic after a car accident at the age of 67. Their experience of their disability will be different, and both these people's needs for accommodations will vary significantly at different times in their lives. The WHO captured this in their 2011 report when they stated that physical disabilities "can be visible or invisible; temporary or long term; static, episodic, or degenerating; painful or inconsequential" (WHO, 2011, p. 8).

People who live with a disability regularly experience social disadvantages. They are more likely to live in poverty, obtain lower levels of education, and often experience social isolation (Australian Human Right Committee, 2016). Importantly for this chapter is the fact that people with physical disabilities are more likely to (repeatedly) be involved with the criminal justice system. This is true for those in the capacity of witnesses, victims, and perpetrators (Australian Human Right Committee, 2016; Dowse et al., 2021). This overrepresentation in the criminal justice system is especially the case for those who are d/Deaf. It has been found that d/Deaf people are especially overrepresented as they are more likely to experience more vulnerabilities than just the physical one (Dowse et al., 2021). As such the majority of this chapter will focus on d/Deaf people as vulnerable suspects.

In general, those who experience bigger and more barriers regarding communication and social ability are more vulnerable during interviews (Powell, 2002. It is exactly these barriers that are prominent amongst people living with disabilities. The consequences are that suspects with physical disabilities are more likely to report unreliable information and/or are more likely to incriminate themselves during police interviews (Powell, 2004). This is an example of how people's access to justice is impacted by their disabilities. The United Nations recognises this impact in the Convention on the Rights of Persons with Disabilities, which states that people with disabilities have a right to obtain effective access to justice. They mandate what is referred to as "reasonable accommodation", which requires that accommodations and/or adjustments are made to remove barriers to effective justice (Australian Human Rights Commission, 2014). These can be visible adjustments, such as making sure police stations, courts, and jails are accessible to those with physical disabilities. They can also include less obvious adjustments such as interpreters for d/Deaf people to ensure they are able to understand and participate in judicial proceedings.

This chapter will start off defining what deafness means, followed by statistics on the d/Deaf population. Next, d/Deaf forms of communication will be addressed and the effect of these on waiving rights. Lastly, an overview of police experience with the d/Deaf population, a case study, and recommendations to standard interview practices are provided.

Defining d/Deaf

Historically the word "deafness" was a medical term which included all degrees of deafness. These were determined by the age of onset, or by what condition it was caused by (Bramley, 2007; Iqbal et al., 2004; Zidenberg et al., 2021). When we dissect the term "deafness", various distinctions can be made. There are distinctions between those that are hard of hearing (HoH), partially, or profoundly d/Deaf. The difference between the three is the onset of hearing loss (e.g., HoH often later in life) and the use of words (e.g., profoundly deaf people have little or no use of verbal language), with partially deaf sitting in between the extremes (Iqbal et al., 2004). Another determinant is the timing that speech was learned. People who experience "prelingual" deafness are those people who were d/Deaf before they could use hearing to learn language, whereas "post-lingual" refers to those people who became d/Deaf after speech acquisition. Generally, those people born d/Deaf (prelingual) will have limited vocabularies, literacy, and verbal language skills (Bramley, 2007; Iqbal et al., 2004). Awareness of these distinctions is important as it will inform how to approach communication during an interview with a suspect who is d/Deaf or HoH.

Another important distinction to be aware of is that between *deaf* (d) and *Deaf* (D). In this distinction deaf (d) represents the medical view and Deaf (D) the socio-cultural view. Deaf (D) people share their own unique language, history, and customs and as such consider themselves part of a cultural minority who take part in the Deaf community (Bramley, 2007; Zidenberg et al., 2021, placing them in another vulnerable position; see Chapter 11, on vulnerabilities of CaLD suspects). Deaf people do not see their deafness as a medical issue, and as such are not inclined to try to "correct" this. When we look at some of the demographic differences between deaf and Deaf people, we see that the latter generally have Deaf parents, and use sign language as their first language (Dennis & Baker, 1998).

Prevalence of d/Deafness

There are more than 70 million people who are d/Deaf in the world according to the United Nations. The vast majority of these (80%) live in developing countries and together they speak more than 300 different sign languages. Even though only a minority of all d/Deaf people live in developed countries (20%), the absolute numbers are still remarkable. For example, Engelman and Deardorff (2016) found that in the United States in 2012 about 36 million people reported to be d/Deaf or hard of hearing (HoH). Similarly, in the UK, 11 million people reportedly have some form of hearing loss (Kelly, 2017; 2108). While the majority of the latter consisted of people who indicated to be HoH, there were still around 900,000 people who were severely and/or culturally d/Deaf. In general, when focusing on congenital d/Deaf people, the European Society for Mental Health and Deafness estimated that about one in 1000 people are born d/Deaf (Iqbal et al., 2004).

Those severely and/or culturally d/Deaf are at a disadvantage within everyday society, as they rely on sign language or have minimal language skills (Bramley, 2007). When people with minimal language skills have to engage with people who do not experience those same limitations with respect to verbal communication, various issues can present. For example, they might not understand questions as they have a poor vocabulary. They are then at risk of providing inappropriate responses to questions, or they might just agree with the questions even if they did not understand what was being asked. These communication barriers become especially pronounced in investigative interviewing situations, where police officers rely on various complex legal terms (e.g., grievous bodily harm), or complicated concepts (e.g., Miranda waiver), amplifying the vulnerability of the d/Deaf people (Miller & Vernon, 2005).

Given these vulnerabilities it is not surprising to see an overrepresentation of d/Deaf people in prisons. There especially seems to be an overrepresentation when it comes to sexual and violent offences (Miller et al., 2005; Zidenberg, 2021). When hearing offenders are compared to those that are d/Deaf, it seems that the only difference between the two is their education, reading, and communication abilities. These differences can all directly be linked to the offenders' d/Deaf status, as d/Deaf people are often deprived of developing and/or obtaining these skills early in life (Zidenberg, 2021). Moreover, the type of crime (i.e., sexual assault) they are convicted of can indirectly be linked to deafness too. For example, Miller et al. (2005) found that d/Deaf people in prison often lack the knowledge of what constitutes illegal sexual behaviour, nor have they had sex education. This is partly caused by the fact that educators and service providers do not know the sign language to communicate about sexual behaviour. Consequently, being unable to learn about appropriate sexual behaviour, or to be effectively asked questions about sexual conduct, has resulted in various wrongful convictions (Miller et al., 2005).

d/Deaf communication

As mentioned at the start of this chapter there is a substantial number of d/Deaf people that rely on sign language for communication. However, there is no universal sign language and—just like spoken language—almost every country has their own sign language. This means there are over 300 different sign languages worldwide (e.g., American Sign Language (ALS); British Sign Language (BLS), etc.; Dennis & Baker, 1998; UN, 2011; Zidenberg, 2021), and there are also dialects within countries (Zidenberg, 2021). While sign languages—like any other language—have their own syntax, grammar, and rules, they cannot be literally translated into spoken languages (Dennis & Baker, 1998; Zidenberg, 2021). There is no written form of sign languages (i.e., you could not translate a BSL sentence in written English without it being confusing), and fluency in a sign language does not predict similar abilities in producing and/or understanding written or spoken language (Dennis & Baker, 1998; Zidenberg, 2021).

An additional challenge is the need for the proper interpretation of paralanguage (e.g., intonation, pitch, and facial expressions) to be able to understand what someone is saying. There are vast differences between spoken and signed languages in terms of paralanguage. For example, d/Deaf people will not rely on tone for emotional expression, but rather exaggerate non-verbal techniques, such as facial expressions, gestures, and body language (Dennis & Baker, 1998). This can come across as artificial behaviour to hearing people. Moreover, touch and sustained eye contact are heavily relied upon by people communicating in sign language. However, these two techniques can cause surprise and suspicion amongst hearing people. d/Deaf people use touch (which can include hugging) to start a conversation, even with people they do not know well (Dennis & Baker, 1998; Kelly, 2017; 2018). Similarly, d/Deaf people will sustain gaze during conversations as they usually rely on that to understand sign language. This intense, uninterrupted gaze can be experienced as uncomfortable or threatening by hearing people (Dennis & Baker, 1998). As such, the non-verbal behaviours that d/Deaf suspects display during interviews may (negatively) influence how they are perceived by the interviewers. This may especially be the case when the latter are not aware of the origin of these behaviours.

In most Western countries laws have been introduced which (amongst others) have legalised the right for people who are d/Deaf to access an interpreter within the legal system (e.g., see Race & Hogue, 2018). However, just because d/Deaf people have the right to an interpreter does not mean there is one available. Availability could be impacted by the sign language ability of the suspect. Specifically, whether they use an officially recognised sign language, a dialect, or they have developed their own signs for communication. There may also be issues in availability more generally due to demand. For example, in the UK there were 883 registered sign language interpreters available for 800,000 d/Deaf people (Race & Hogue, 2018). This can create real problems. In the past, family members (even young children) have been asked to interpret when no accredited interpreter was available. Besides the ethical issues with having a family member interpret a police interview, there are also concerns with the quality of interpretation and consequently the understanding by the suspect (Race & Hogue, 2015).

Speech- or lip-reading is not a reliable form of communication with d/Deaf people (Bramley, 2007; Dennis & Baker, 1998). Speech reading is heavily impacted by the distance between the speaker and the reader, the presence of any facial hair, and the ability to speech read by the d/Deaf person (Bramley, 2007; Dennis & Baker, 1998). In the current climate where masks are commonly worn due to COVID-19, additional difficulty is experienced by people who may, at least to some extent, rely on speech reading.

Police experience with d/Deaf people

Police themselves report mixed feelings regarding their experiences with the d/Deaf community. When it comes down to basic facts, Zidenberg (2021) reported that only few departments in the United States kept records on their interactions with d/Deaf people, while about one third have official policies directing how to engage with victims, witnesses, and suspects who are d/Deaf. However, many of the policies include problematic practices mentioned in this chapter, such as handcuffing suspects' hands behind their backs. Similarly, in Australia, there are reports that police fail to call interpreters due to the costs and effort involved (Human Rights Committee (HRC), 2014). Police often have false beliefs about the abilities of people who are d/Deaf (e.g., that they can speech read), or misinterpret their lack of response to instructions as aggression (HRC, 2014). A very persistent misunderstanding amongst some police around the world is that when a person who is d/Deaf nods this is a sign of understanding. In reality this is an action people who are d/Deaf perform when they actually do not understand what is said or asked (Bramley, 2007). Zidenberg et al. (2021) showed that these misunderstandings of behaviour and comprehension can have severe consequences for d/Deaf suspects including "wrongful conviction, important evidence being excluded due to improper procedures, and negative perceptions of police that impede victims from coming forward" (p. 376). As such training more widely would benefit both the police and d/Deaf people.

Implications for interviews

Waiving rights

d/Deaf people seem to be at an extreme disadvantage in the legal system, purely based on the procedures used. In most countries, when a person is arrested, their hands need to be handcuffed, often behind their backs (Vernon & Miller, 2005). Given that many d/Deaf people rely on sign language to communicate, this means they are prevented from communicating. At the same time, the arrest and being processed into custody can create anxiety and fear, even when the person is innocent. d/Deaf people cannot hear what is being said, and consequently cannot comprehend what is happening or what they are accused of (Vernon et al., 1996). This fear may cause a person who is d/Deaf to do anything that they think will get them out of the threatening situation, including signing papers, or confessing to crimes (Vernon et al., 1996). Further, police officers are considered authority figures which may make a person who is d/Deaf more likely to comply with their requests, even if it concerns signing forms they do not comprehend (Vernon & Miller, 2005). This is especially relevant when it comes to the caution/Miranda warnings.

As mentioned in Chapters 8 and 11, cautions and Miranda rights are grammatically and legally complex, and difficult to understand for suspects who are able to hear. Given the complexity, one option proposed for d/Deaf suspects is to provide them with a written caution. However, researchers have shown that for proper understanding of cautions, a tenth-grade reading level is needed (Vernon & Miller, 2005). Research has found that a typical person who is d/Deaf has the reading ability of a fourth grader (Zidenberg, 2021). Moreover, prelingual d/Deaf people, who are fluent in sign language, but who have not heard spoken languages, may lack the competence to understand a written caution, particularly because it is not in their first language. It is important to note that fluency in sign language does not mean the person will have similar abilities in written and spoken languages. Interestingly, research has shown that people in general who cannot read properly are actually used to signing forms they do not understand (Vernon, 1996; Zidenberg, 2021). As a result, a person who is d/Deaf may sign a waiver when presented by an officer without fully comprehending what the waiver means, or stands for.

Signing (in sign language) the caution is the best option. However, this can be challenging too. As mentioned above, there is no literal translation for sign language and as such the nuances of cautions can be difficult to convey in signs (Zidenberg, 2021). As such, additional steps can be taken to securely support the suspect and safeguard the process. Vernon and Miller (2005) stated that the entire interrogation including administering the cautions should be videotaped. All people should be visible in this tape and especially their upper bodies, including hands. This way, full signs can be captured and the translation can later be evaluated for accuracy and completeness, protecting the validity of the administration of the caution.

Interview guidelines

When interviewing a suspect who is d/Deaf, the following steps should be taken:

- Engage a qualified interpreter. As outlined in this chapter, the content and complexity of an interview means that you should not rely on reading abilities of the suspect, nor on an untrained interpreter. Never use family members, or rely on speech reading (Vernon et al., 2001).
- Pay attention when setting up an interview. Make sure the interpreter and the suspect can understand each other. Give the interpreter time (at least 15 minutes of signing) to assess the sign language abilities of the suspect. If they are inadequate, do not proceed with the interview (Dennis & Baker, 1998, Vernon et al., 2001). Ask the interpreter if they can understand the suspect, and assess from the suspect if they are comfortable with the interpreter and can understand them. Explain that the interview will be video recorded and that those recordings can be used in court (Vernon et al., 2001).
- Reading rights. Discuss with the interpreter if they believe the suspect will understand the reading of their rights. Make sure that the interpreters get the suspect to re-sign each section of their rights in their own words/sign to confirm comprehension (Vernon et al., 2001).
- Checking. Check throughout the interview that the communication between the interpreter and the suspect is adequate. If there is any doubt about the quality of the communication, stop the interview as evidence can be lost or dismissal of the case can happen when the interview is questioned in court (Vernon et al., 2001).

Case study

Training programs to help police officers communicate with d/Deaf people have been developed and evaluated around the world (Engelman & Deardorff, 2016; Race & Hough, 2018; Zidenberg, 2021). For example, the Police Link Officers for Deaf People (PLOD) scheme was introduced in the UK in 1991. The main feature of this program focuses on designated officers receiving awareness, and basic sign language training. The intention is for police officers to use these skills in order to become the link between the police and the d/Deaf community. This would assure that when d/Deaf people come to the police station they are able to communicate with someone (Race & Hogue, 2018). However, some convincing is still needed for the d/Deaf community, who are sceptical about the abilities of, and interactions with, the police officers after training (Zidenberg, 2021).

Other options to accommodate d/Deaf people during the custodial process have been proposed. For example, it has been proposed to administer the caution using speech reading. As mentioned above, speech reading is often considered to be a reliable form of communication with d/Deaf people (Bramley, 2007; Denni s& Baker, 1998). However, this is far from true. Speech reading in actuality, is extremely difficult, especially in English. This is due to the fact that two thirds of the sounds used in the English language are actually not visible on the lips (Vernon et al., 1996). For hearing people, this would mean listening to sentences with two thirds of each word inaudible. When looking at speech readers who are d/Deaf, research has found that they only understand 5% of what is said, even under ideal visual circumstances (Vernon et al., 1996). The inefficiency of speech reading becomes even more apparent when the world's best speech readers only understand about one quarter of what is spoken to them (Vernon et al., 1996). While would not be expected a person to understand a caution in a foreign language they do not properly speak, People who are d/Deaf in these situations may be expected to (Vernon et al., 1996). Considering these numbers, it becomes glaringly clear that speech reading should not be used to communicate cautions/Miranda rights.

Conclusion

People with physical disabilities are vulnerable during suspect interviews. This is especially true when it comes to d/Deaf people. Those suspects that identify as Deaf (D) should be considered especially vulnerable as they consider themselves part of a cultural minority, due to their own language, customs, and history. Given the essential role of language throughout the custodial process it is pertinent that d/Deaf suspects are able to communicate. This means they might need their hands to sign, and they have a right to an interpreter. Do not rely on speech-/lip-reading with a d/Deaf suspect as it has been shown to be unreliable at best.

Acknowledge that fluency in sign language does not translate to written or spoken language. Moreover, there is no literal translation from sign language to spoken language. This is especially important when it comes to cautions and interpreting information provided by the d/Deaf suspect. Be prepared for unexpected paralanguage which relies on touch and can involve extended gaze. This is part of natural paralanguage amongst d/Deaf people and should be considered as such. Incorporate the above guidelines when interviewing d/Deaf suspects and especially focus on repeated comprehension checks. This will facilitate as well as protect the integrity of interview with a d/Deaf suspect.

References

Australian Human Rights Commission (2014). *Equal before the law: Towards disability justice strategies*. Australian Human Rights Commission.

Australian Human Rights Commission (2016). *Equal before the law? How the criminal justice system is failing people with disability*. Australian Human Rights Commission.

Bartels, L. (2011). *Police interviews with vulnerable adult suspects*. The Australian Institute of Criminology

Bramley, S. (2007). Working with deaf people who have committed sexual offences against children: The need for an increased awareness. *Journal of Sexual Aggression, 13*(1), 59–69.

Dennis, M.J., & Baker, K.A. (1998). Evaluation and treatment of deaf sexual offenders. In *Sourcebook of treatment programs for sexual offenders* (pp. 287–302). Springer.

Dowse, L., Rowe, S., Baldry, E., & Baker, M. (2021). *Police responses to people with disability*.

Engelman, A., & Deardorff, J. (2016). Cultural competence training for law enforcement responding to domestic violence emergencies with the deaf and hard of hearing: A mixed-methods evaluation. *Health Promotion Practice, 17*(2), 177–185.

Iqbal, S., Dolan, M.C., & Monteiro, B.T. (2004). Characteristics of deaf sexual offenders referred to a specialist mental health unit in the UK. *Journal of Forensic Psychiatry & Psychology, 15*(3), 494–510.

Kelly, L. (2017). Suffering in silence: The unmet needs of d/Deaf prisoners. *Prison Service Journal, 234*, 3–15.

Kelly, L.M. (2018). Sounding out d/deafness: The experiences of d/deaf prisoners. *Journal of Criminal Psychology. 8*(1), 20–32

Miller, K.R., Vernon, M., & Capella, M.E. (2005). Violent offenders in a deaf prison population. *Journal of Deaf Studies and Deaf Education, 10*(4), 417–425

Powell, M. B. (2002). Specialist training in investigative and evidential interviewing: Is it having any effect on the behaviour of professionals in the field?. *Psychiatry, Psychology and Law, 9*(1), 44–55.

Race, L., & Hogue, T.E. (2018). 'You have the right to remain silent' Current provisions for D/deaf people within regional police forces in England and Wales. *Police Journal, 91*(1), 64–88.

Vernon, M., & Miller, K. (2005). Obstacles faced by deaf people in the criminal justice system. *American Annals of the Deaf, 150*(3), 283–291.

Vernon, M., Raifman, L.J., & Greenberg, S.F. (1996). The Miranda warnings and the deaf suspect. *Behavioral Sciences & the Law, 14*(1), 121–135.

Vernon, M., Raifman, L.J., Greenberg, S.F., & Monteiro, B. (2001). Forensic pretrial police interviews of deaf suspects avoiding legal pitfalls. *International Journal of Law and Psychiatry*, 24(1), 43–59.

World Health Organization. (2011). *World report on disability*. World Health Organization. Available at: www.who.int. Accessed March 2022.

Zidenberg, A.M. (2021). Avoiding the deaf penalty: a review of the experiences of d/Deaf individuals in the criminal justice system. *Disability & Society*, 1–23.

Zidenberg, A.M., Rine, S.S., & Olver, M. (2021). Correctional and forensic contexts of d/Deaf persons: implications for assessment and treatment. *Journal of Offender Rehabilitation*, 60(6), 375–394.

Conclusion

Police interviewing is a key inquisitorial component of the criminal justice systems that exist in many jurisdictions across the world (Williamson, 1993; van Koppen & Penrod, 2003). The interview process and outcomes have substantial implications for the prosecution and defence of an accused person. The absence of adequate accommodations made for vulnerabilities during interviews can result in unjust outcomes. Bearing these significant considerations in mind, this book set about exploring the ways in which vulnerability (both general and specific) can impact a suspect in the interview context and provided strategies for use by police in interviews.

Vulnerability

At the outset of this book, the argument was made that all individuals who come into contact with the criminal justice system are, by virtue of that contact alone, vulnerable. What has typically been denoted as specific vulnerabilities—those additional factors such as intellectual impairment, intoxication, age and cultural diversity—add additional layer(s) onto what we might term assumed vulnerability.

Following miscarriages of justice in the United Kingdom in the 1980s which prompted the introduction of an investigative approach to interviewing, significant interviewing reform took place internationally. However, difficulty interviewing vulnerable suspects continues to result in public miscarriages of this type, although they appear to be rarer. More common are circumstances where police officers feel ill-equipped to conduct interviews with suspects who may be vulnerable, raising questions about how to determine whether someone is vulnerable, and what to do once such a determination has been made.

Formal interventions, for example, custody screening, will assist in identifying psychological vulnerability, but will not necessarily assist in identifying any other form of vulnerability that might impact the manner in which an interview is conducted or the outcomes of said interview. Throughout Part II of this book, we considered specific vulnerabilities and provided guidelines with respect to conducting interviews with suspects who may be exhibiting signs of that specific vulnerability. However, in considering an overarching approach to take with respect to interviewing vulnerable suspects (or suspects who may be vulnerable), we have emphasised the importance of rapport building and planning.

In Chapter 2, rapport building was identified as key to identifying vulnerability. While some vulnerabilities may be identifiable through file notes from previous interactions with police, or intelligence from other sources, some vulnerabilities will only be identified once the suspect begins interacting with police, and others only by disclosure. To that end, being observant and intentional in rapport building and maintenance, from the first interaction, is essential in determining potential vulnerabilities as early as possible in the process. Those invisible vulnerabilities that will only become apparent by disclosure are more likely to be disclosed if the suspect feels comfortable enough, which can be achieved during the rapport building phase. In some circumstances, a specific vulnerability may not become apparent until the commencement of the interview, or sometime during the interview. When this occurs, it is appropriate to pause the interview in order to plan how best to proceed. Having established the importance of rapport building in identifying vulnerability, in Chapter 2 we also highlighted that planning, once a vulnerability is known or suspected, is necessary to ensure that the manner in which the interview is conducted minimises the impact of the vulnerability on the integrity of the interview process.

What do we do with this information?

Part II of this book has been designed to provide an understanding of various specific vulnerabilities that may be encountered by police in interviews with suspects. Each chapter considered a different vulnerability and outlined suggestions for interviewing suspects who experience that particular vulnerability. Importantly, people may experience multiple vulnerabilities and this will need to be considered carefully in planning if and how to proceed with an interview.

For police officers to effectively interview vulnerable suspects, they need to possess skills in rapport building and planning, as well as have an understanding of the way in which specific vulnerabilities may impact the interview process. Specialised interview training is a feature of police training in jurisdictions around the world. As discussed in Chapter 4, some jurisdictions offer a tiered approach to training, providing training for more complex interviewing skills as police officers gain more experience. Rapport building and planning are likely to form part of most basic interview training, and will certainly form part of training in the PEACE model of interviewing. These "soft skills" are not necessarily innate, but they can be taught. Ideally, strategies for interviewing vulnerable suspects would also form part of introductory interviewing training. In discussing the role of supervision in Chapter 5, the authors highlighted the way in which supervision can impact interviewing skill development and maintenance. Quality assurance can be attained through regular supervision and assessment of interviewing competencies.

A final note

Ultimately, many of the suggestions contained within this book for use in interviews with vulnerable suspects are not particularly arduous and could be applied to interviewing more generally. Doing so would firstly recognise the inherent vulnerability of a suspect in the criminal justice system, and secondly ensure that suspects whose specific vulnerability is invisible and undisclosed are less likely to be disadvantaged by the interview process.

In the Introduction, readers were provided with an extract of Justice Forster's judgement in *Anunga v R* (1976) ALR 412. The guidelines presented in that judgement can be applied to all interviews with vulnerable suspects and, as suggested above, suspects generally. These guidelines were referred to in Chapter 11 (Culturally and Linguistically Diverse and First Nations suspects). Remembering that their initial publication was in 1976 and in reference to a specific group, the following list is an adaptation for a generalised approach recognising the inherent vulnerability of suspects:

1. An interpreter should be utilised where the suspect is not able to understand or communicate in English.
2. A "prisoner's friend" or support person should be present.
3. Be careful when administering the caution and ask the suspect to explain the caution in their own words to check their understanding.
4. Ask non-leading questions and be mindful of tone and manner to avoid indicating a preferred response.
5. Confessions must be corroborated.
6. Provide fluids, food, and the opportunity for comfort breaks.
7. Do not interview a suspect who is "disabled by illness or drunkenness or tiredness" (p. 415) or question a suspect for an unreasonable length of time.
8. Assist in securing legal advice and/or stop the interview when requested.
9. If clothing is removed for a forensic procedure, ensure replacement clothing is provided.

Paraphrasing Justice Forster, these guidelines are not designed to be offensive to, or unfairly favour, suspects. However, they recognise the particular disadvantage faced by some, and are an attempt to alleviate this in the context of a police interview. Increasing fairness for vulnerable suspects ultimately increases the likelihood of justice for all.

References

Anunga v R (1976) ALR 412.

Van Koppen, P.J., & Penrod, S.D. (2003). *Adversarial versus inquisitorial justice: Psychological perspectives on criminal justice systems*. Kluwer Academic/Plenum Publishers.

Williamson, T.M. (1993). From interrogation to investigative interviewing: Strategic trends in police questioning. *Journal of Community and Applied Social Psychology, 3*, 89–99. doi: 10.1002/casp.2450030203

Index

Note: Page numbers in *italics* indicate figures, **bold** indicate tables in the text, and references following "n" refer notes

Aboriginal and Torres Strait Islander peoples 2, 80, 84–85; cultural and socio-economic backgrounds amongst 81; investigative interview with 84–86; vulnerability in police interviewing 2
accommodations for vulnerabilities 63, 72, 75–76, 80, 95–96
"Account" phase 15, 17, 25, 78
acculturation 84–86
Achieving Best Evidence (ABE) 25–29, 32
addiction 8, 48
admissibility 1, 7, 28, 45, 75
age/ageing 8, 12, 52–54; of child witnesses 59; of older offenders 52, 54; of suspect 55, 61, 62, 90; vulnerability due to 76
alcohol: consumption 45, 46; withdrawal 48
Alzheimer disease 52–56
antidepressants 46
Appropriate Adult (AA) 19–20, 62–63, 69, 76
Asperger's Syndrome 74
attention 7, 8, 10, 11, 14–15, 17, 24; impaired 48; potential for cognitive decline 52; on witnesses 47
Attention Deficit Hyperactivity Disorder (ADHD) 74
Autism Spectrum Disorder (ASD) 3, 72, 74–75; guidelines for interviewing suspect with 78; implications for interviewing suspect with 77; organisations 74; personal experience with 75

BARS-PEACE 36
behaviourally anchored rating scale (BARS) 36
benzodiazepines 46
body language 56, 98
Breathalyser tests 48–49
Brief Jail Mental Health Screen 67
British Sign Language (BLS) 97

cautions 60, 73, 75, 77, 81, 83, 99–101
children as suspects *see* juvenile suspects
cisheteronormative culture 90

"Closure" 15, 25, 27, 29, 78
cognitive impairment 8, 75
Cognitive Interview 77, 78
cognitive load in suspects 10, 21, 47
collectivist cultures 83–84
complication proportions 21–22
Convention on Rights of Persons with Disabilities 25, 96
crimes 45–46, 59, 61, 97; committed by older offenders 53, 54, 56; interviewing suspect of 84; mock 47, 48
criminal justice processes 73
criminal justice system 2, 7, 76, 81; older adult suspects in 52, 53; overrepresentation in 74, 95–96; people with ASD contact with 74; people with physical disabilities in 95; prevalence of people with ID in 72; vulnerability in 8–11
Crisis Intervention Team training (CIT training) 67–68
Culturally and Linguistically Diverse suspects (CaLD suspects) 10, 80; case study 86; implications for interviews with people 83–84; interpreters 82–83; relationship between CaLD peoples and police 81–82

d/Deaf people 95–96; case study 100–101; communication 97–98; implications for interviews 99–100; police experience with 98–99; population 97
Deafblind Woman Who Conquered Harvard Law, The (Girma) 30
deinstitutionalisation 7–8
delirium 48
dementia 52, 54–56
depression 48, 54
disability 8, 73, 95; cognitive 72; invisible 74, 75
domestic violence 54
drinking 54
drug use 48, 54

Index

echo questions 26
empathy 14, 28, 31, 35, 78
"Engage and explain" phase of interview 13–15, 17, 28, 78, 91
English as a second language (ESL) 81
European Convention on Human Rights (ECHR) 82
executive functioning 45

First Nations peoples: Australians and Canadians 81; implications for interviews with 84–86; relationship with police 84
Foetal Alcohol Spectrum Disorder (FASD) 1, 3, 72–74; guidelines for interviewing suspect with 77–78; implications for interviewing suspect with 76–77
Framework of Investigate Transformation (FIT) 37, 38
"free narrative" phase of interview 28, 85

gender 89–90; contemporary police culture 91–92; historical attitudes towards LGBTQIA+ community 90–91; identity 8, 90; implications for interviews 92–93; police training 92

hard of hearing (HoH) 96–97
hearing impairment: case study 100–101; d/Deaf 96–99; implications for interviews 99–100
homelessness 8, 72
Human Rights Committee (HRC) 98

individualistic cultures 83–84
inhibition 45, 47, 50, 56, 72, 84
intellectual and learning impairments 72; ASD 74–75; FASD 73–74
intellectual disabilities (ID) 72–73, 75–76
International Covenant on Civil and Political Rights (ICCPR) 82
interviewees 13, 22, 28, 35; cultural background of 84; rapport with 15, 16, 85; witness reluctance, or power differential of 14
interviewers 21, 27, 61; accompanying 29; lead 16, 29; police 19, 20, 25, 26, 28, 34, 36, 65; principles for 13; rapport with 15; self-assessment 35; skilled 28; tier 3 interviewer 35–36
interviewer training 24; "Closure" phase of interview 29; "Engage and explain" phase of interview 28; interviewing style 31; PEACE model 25; phased approach 27; planning 27; presence at interviews of advisors 30–31; proportion of suspects 24; questioning 28–29; research on interviewing skills 26; UN guidance 30
interview guidelines 26; CaLD and First Nations peoples, for interviewing 84–86; d/Deaf people, for interviewing 100; for encouraging inclusive use of pronouns 93; intoxicated suspects, for interviewing 49–50; juvenile suspects, for interviewing 61–62; mental illness, for interviewing suspects with 68–69; older adult suspects, for interviewing 55–56
interview supervision and management 34–38
intoxication 45; AOD and crime in numbers 46; case study 50; implications for interviews 48–50; interactions with, and perceptions of, intoxicated suspects 46; vulnerabilities of intoxicated suspects 46–48

juvenile suspects 3, 31, 58, 59; case study 62–63; developmental vulnerabilities 58–59; implications for interviews 59–62; interview guidelines 61–62; suggestibility 59–60

knowledge details, common 22

Law Society in the United Kingdom 93
Lesbian, Gay, Bisexual, Transsexual, Questioning, Intersex, and Asexual+ (LGBTQIA+) 89; historical attitudes towards 90–91; police liaison officers 92
Liaison and Diversion teams (LD teams) 69
lip-reading 98, 101

Mendez Principles 34, 38
meso level factors 38
micro-level factors 38
MIND (Mental Health Charity) 69
Miranda rights 47, 60, 99, 101
miscarriages of justice 11, 103
mock theft paradigm 28

National College of Policing 26
neutrality 38, 83
non-verbal behaviours 17, 98

older adults 52–53; crimes of 54–55; Dementia and Alzheimer's impact in 56
older offenders 53–54; implications for interviews 55–56; perceptions of older offenders 54–55
on-call MIND volunteer 69–70
"one-size-fits-all" approach 65
over-policing 72, 82
oversight mechanisms 39

PACE Act 70
paralanguage 95, 98, 101
parent–child interactions 84
perceptions: of older offenders 54–55; of people with mental illness 66; of procedural justice 66
phased approach 27
Planning and preparation; Account, clarification, and challenge; and Evaluation model (PEACE model) 25, 34, 59, 65, 78, 91; effectiveness 15; implementation 13; of interviewing 11, 104; phases 25
Police and Criminal Evidence Act 1984 8, 19, 38, 63

police experience with d/Deaf people 98–99
police interviewers 19, 20, 25, 26, 28, 34, 36, 65
police interviewing/interviews 1, 8, 26, 34, 36, 37, 103; in England and Wales 25; evaluations of audio-recorded, real-life interviews 34; people with mental health disorders 26; role of lawyer in 20, 30; suggestibility in 59; suspect's mental illness impacting 3; vulnerability in 2
Police Link Officers for Deaf People scheme (PLOD scheme) 100
post-lingual deafness 96
"prelingual" deafness 96
"preparation and planning" phase of interview 13
prior knowledge, rapport, interpretive assistance, diverse array of hypotheses, effective techniques (PRIDE techniques) 85
psychological vulnerability 12, 25, 52, 56, 65–66, 103

quality assurance 82–83, 104

rapport-based interviewing 13
rapport building 12, 13, 31, 36, 56, 85, 103–104; components of 14; in investigative interviews 14–16, 89; rapport phase of interviews 28; strategies for establishment with vulnerable suspects 16–17
"Reid Technique" 36
right to legal advice 21

self-incrimination 59–61
self-restraint 84

sexual diversity 89–90; contemporary police culture 91–92; historical attitudes towards LGBTQIA+ community 90–91; implications for interviews 92–93; police training 92
Shaw, G. 31
sign languages 95–100
SPECTRUM database 69
speech reading 98, 100, 101
strategic use of evidence method (SUE method) 21
suggestibility 37, 45, 48, 58, 61, 72; interrogative 59, 60, 76, 77; of juvenile suspects 59–60; reduction 77
sustained eye contact 98

third party interviewing 19, 30; intermediaries 19–20; interpreters 21–22; lawyers 20–21; strategies for 22
tier 3 interviewers 35–36
tier 5 role in UK 35–36
touch technique 98, 101

United Nations guidance (UN guidance) 30

violent/violence 72; alcohol consumption increases risk of 46; crimes 46; domestic 54; intimate partner 91
voice, tone of 16, 38, 56

waiving rights 60, 76, 99
Williamson, T. 25
World Health Organization (WHO) 53, 95

Printed in the United States
by Baker & Taylor Publisher Services